W9-CPB-279

AMERICAN
★ ★ ★ ★ ★ ★ ★ ★ ★ ★ ★ ★
TRIVIA

Publications International, Ltd.

Cover art: Art Explosion, Getty, Shutterstock.com

Interior art: Art Explosion: 10, 23, 52, 169, 174; **Clipart.com:** 9, 12, 13; Getty: 154, 180, 202; **Publications International, Ltd.:** 202; **Shutterstock**.com: 14, 32, 45, 54, 58, 69, 73, 78, 81, 87, 90, 91, 93, 95, 103, 104, 105, 109, 117, 122, 124, 130, 137, 138, 141, 144, 145, 146, 147, 155, 157, 159, 160, 161, 164, 166, 170, 172, 178, 181, 182, 183, 185, 186, 203, 204, 213, 216, 217, 218, 228, 234, 237, 240, 242, 245, 246, 249, 251, 252, 253, 254, 259, 264, 266, 271

Louis Weber, CEO
Publications International, Ltd.
7373 North Cicero Avenue
Lincolnwood, Illinois 60712

Permission is never granted for commercial purposes.

ISBN: 978-1-68022-174-9

Manufactured in Canada.

8 7 6 5 4 3 2 1

Contents

Exploration and Discovery

Q. How did the Pilgrims get to the New World?

A. When the Pilgrims began their voyage to the New World, they didn't expect to sail on the *Mayflower*, nor did they plan to land at Plymouth Rock.

Destination: Holland

The story of the Pilgrims begins back in 1606, 14 years before they set sail on the *Mayflower*.

A band of worshippers from Scrooby Manor, who belonged to the Church of England, decided that they would rather worship God according to the Bible than indulge in the extra prayers and hymns imposed by the church. However, separating from the church was easier said than done. In England, it was illegal to be a Separatist. Risking imprisonment, the worshippers escaped to Holland, a land of religious tolerance. But their time in Holland was a mixed blessing. Although they worshipped freely, they feared their children were becoming more Dutch than English.

Destination: Hudson River

Meanwhile, English noblemen were seeking brave, industrious people to sail to America and establish colonies in Virginia (which extended far beyond the Virginia we know today). They offered the Separatists a contract for land at the mouth of the Hudson River, near present-day New York City.

Led by William Brewster and William Bradford, the Separatists accepted the offer and began preparing for their voyage. They even bought their own boat, the *Speedwell*. In July 1620, they sailed to England to meet 52 more passengers who rode in their own ship, the *Mayflower*. The Separatists, who called themselves "Saints," referred to these new people as "Strangers."

Destination: Unknown

The *Speedwell* should have been called the *Leakwell*. After two disastrous starts, the Saints abandoned hope of her sailing again. On September 6, they joined the Strangers on the *Mayflower*.

The *Mayflower* was just 30 yards long—about the length of three school buses. The 50 Saints rode in the "tween" deck, an area between the two decks that was actually the gun deck. Its ceilings were only about five feet high.

Accommodations in the rest of the boat were hardly better. Cramped into close quarters were 52 Strangers, 30 crewmen (who laughed at the seasick landlubbers), 2 dogs (a spaniel and a mastiff), barley, oats, shovels, hammers, tools, beer, cheese, cooking pots, and chamber pots. There may have been pigs on board, too.

As they journeyed across the Atlantic, storms and rough waters pushed them off course. After 65 days on the high seas, they realized they were nowhere near the Hudson River. Instead, they sighted the finger of Cape Cod—more than 220 miles away from their destination.

Though they were far from the land contracted for the English colony, the settlers saw their arrival in the New World as an opportunity to build a better life. In November 1620, 41 free men (Saints and Strangers alike) signed the Mayflower Compact. They agreed to work together for the good of the colony and to elect leaders to create a "civil body politic."

But What About Plymouth Rock?
After anchoring in a harbor (which is now Provincetown), the Saints formed three expeditions to locate a suitable place to live. One expedition ventured 30 miles west to a place called "Plimouth," which had been mapped several years earlier by explorer John Smith.

The settlers first noticed a giant rock, probably weighing 200 tons, near the shore. The land nearby had already been cleared. Likely, more than a thousand Native people had lived there before being wiped out by an epidemic. Some remaining bones were still visible.

In December 1620, the group decided to make Plymouth its settlement. According to legend, each passenger stepped on Plymouth Rock upon landing. If this actually happened, leader William Bradford did not record it.

By springtime, half of the *Mayflower*'s passengers would be dead. Yet their accomplishments remain important. Helped by Native people, the Saints and Strangers would live and work together to form one of the first British settlements in North America.

Q. How long did it take Nellie Bly to travel around the world?

A. Nellie Bly gained fame as an undercover reporter, writing an exposé on an asylum in New York that brought about reforms in mental-health care. However, she is best known for her 1889 attempt to travel around the world in less than 80 days, surpassing the hero of

Jules Verne's popular novel. She beat the fictional Phileas Fogg with a round-the-world time of 72 days, 6 hours, 11 minutes, and 14 seconds.

Q. Where in the modern-day United States did Christopher Columbus land?

A. Nowhere. It's a common myth that Columbus sailed to the United States when he "discovered" America, but at no time in his life did Christopher Columbus lay eyes on any of what are today's 50 United States. He did visit Puerto Rico, however, and named the Virgin Islands. His only visit to the American landmass was on his fourth voyage—when he cruised from modern Honduras to Panama.

Q. Where is the oldest continuous European settlement in the United States?

A. St. Augustine, Florida. Because Florida was not one of the original 13 colonies and did not join the United States until the 19th century, St. Augustine is often left out of a discussion of America's first cities. First spotted in 1513 by Spanish explorer Ponce de León, the site of present-day St. Augustine was an important site in the colonial battles between France, England, and Spain. France sent a convoy to settle the east coast of Florida, right in the path of Spain's treasure ships returning home with plunder from the New World. In August 1565, Pedro

Menéndez de Avilés, a Spanish admiral, destroyed French forces stationed there and built the town of St. Augustine—some 40 years before the British settled Jamestown, Virginia.

Q. What did the Puritans do with their corncobs?

A. Colonial Americans ate a lot of corn. Cornmeal pudding, cornmeal pancakes, and plain old cornmeal mush were served up three times a day, along with the occasional side dish of roasted corn, boiled corn, and even popped corn. When you eat that much corn, you're going to end up with a lot of corncobs.

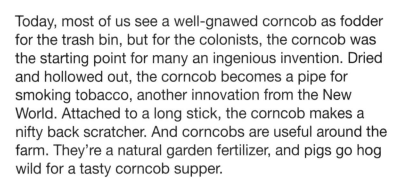

Today, most of us see a well-gnawed corncob as fodder for the trash bin, but for the colonists, the corncob was the starting point for many an ingenious invention. Dried and hollowed out, the corncob becomes a pipe for smoking tobacco, another innovation from the New World. Attached to a long stick, the corncob makes a nifty back scratcher. And corncobs are useful around the farm. They're a natural garden fertilizer, and pigs go hog wild for a tasty corncob supper.

But there's another, even more valuable service that the humble corncob performed for those industrious early Americans. We'll spare you a vivid description, but let's just say that today we'd much rather reach for a roll of soft, quilted paper to do it. That's right—outhouses in cosmopolitan cities like Boston and Philadelphia were stocked with stacks of cobs placed near the wooden seat. In more rustic settings, people kept a pile by the back door of the house, making it easy to slip one into your pocket before walking into the woods for privacy.

Why corncobs? They're slightly more absorbent than leaves, straw, or other readily available natural materials. True, they're not a particularly desirable substitute for the "squeezably soft" paper products marketed today, but paper was in short supply in the colonies. It was used primarily for printed matter that was intended for the ages and sages, and it was rarely discarded.

All that changed in 1704 with the debut of the *Boston News-Letter*, America's first continuously published newspaper. Started as a one-page weekly, it soon expanded to four pages. By 1719, the *News-Letter* had a competitor, the *Boston Gazette*, another multi-page weekly. It didn't take the good citizens of Boston long to find out that last week's paper could be put to good use as a wiping instrument.

No one knows the identity of the enterprising soul who first brought a copy of the *News-Letter* or *Gazette* into the outhouse. Perhaps it was someone who just wanted to sit and read, and having finished with both the paper and the call of nature, was seized with a truly brilliant inspiration. The answer is buried in the annals of history, but toilet paper rolls on.

Q. Which of the 13 colonies was founded by fishermen?

A. New Hampshire, which, ironically, has just 18 miles of shoreline, the least amount of any coastal colony or state—then and now. David Thompson and his partners were given a British land grant on November 15,

1622, and they settled at the mouth of the Piscataqua River, at a place that is today called Odiorne's Point in Rye. Thompson named the settlement Pannaway Plantation, and its purpose was entirely commercial—it was intended to survive through fishing and fur trapping.

Q. How did North and South America get their names?

A. The continents may have been named after Italian explorer Amerigo Vespucci, who made as many as four voyages to South America between 1497 and 1504. On a 1501 trek, he realized he wasn't visiting Asia, as Columbus had believed, but a brand-spankin' new continent. He wrote about his exploits (livening them up with salacious details of native behavior wherever he felt necessary) in a series of letters to his patrons. German cartographer Martin Waldseemüller, a fan, decided to label the new land *America* on a 1507 map. The answer above, however, said the continents "may have been" named for him. Some historians contend that the term *America* was already in use at the time and that Waldseemüller was incorrect in assuming it referred to Vespucci. No matter where the name originated, however, Waldseemüller's intention was to honor Vespucci. This map proved highly influential, as other cartographers began to use *America* as well, and before long, it had stuck.

Q. Whom did President Thomas Jefferson hire to explore the newly bought Louisiana Territory?

A. William Clark and Meriwether Lewis. The duo set out in May 1804 to explore and map the American West. Accompanied by a crew of explorers, they traveled from Missouri to the Oregon coast and back. Their 8,000-mile journey took two years, four months, and ten days.

Q. Who is responsible for the settlement of Kentucky?

A. Daniel Boone. Boone recorded much about his exploration and settlement of Kentucky in his published personal account, *The Adventures of Daniel Boone*. His first expedition into the region took place in 1767, and he later colonized the area at the site of Boonesborough in April 1775. When he brought another party westward later that year, it included his family and solidified his role as a leader of Kentucky settlement.

Q. Who discovered the remains of the *Titanic*?

A. Robert Ballard. Expeditions from around the world searched for the wreckage in the North Atlantic, but it remained elusive until Ballard, an American undersea explorer, discovered it in 1985. In 1986, Ballard made the first detailed study of the ship, producing an in-depth photographic record of one of the most infamous disasters of the 20th century.

Q. **During their expedition across the American West in 1804–1806, explorers Meriwether Lewis and William Clark were accompanied by a French fur trader and his young Shoshone wife. What was her name?**

A. Sacagawea. Although she did not serve as a guide for the expedition, as is often reported, Sacagawea helped foster diplomacy with Native Americans, provided input on the best routes to take, and served as an interpreter.

Q. **Who was the first person to reach the North Pole?**

A. Robert E. Peary and Matthew Henson. Although most people recognize the name Robert Peary, he wasn't alone when he arrived at the North Pole in 1909. He was accompanied by Matthew Henson, an African American who was often dismissed as Peary's servant but who was finally recognized as codiscoverer and awarded a joint medal by Congress in 1944. Also with Peary and Henson at the pole were four Inuit guides.

Q. Whose autobiography is titled *Alone*?

A. Admiral Richard A. Byrd. Byrd was a naval officer and pioneering American aviator and explorer who flew over the North and South Poles and traveled to Antarctica six times. His autobiography details, among other adventures, his solitary five-month stay in a meteorological station in Antarctica, during which he almost died of carbon monoxide poisoning.

Q. What happened to the Donner Party?

A. Starting around 1845, hundreds of thousands of Americans migrated west, believing that it was their "manifest destiny" to claim that territory and seek their fortunes. The story of the Donner Party is one of the most tragic tales in U.S. history.

A New Frontier
To reach Oregon and California, settlers had to cross the Great Plains, a journey that took weeks to complete. There was little water or shelter on this vast expanse of land, and many travelers died of dehydration, cholera, or pneumonia.

In April 1846, George Donner formed a group of 33 people (mostly members of his family) to head west to Sutter's Fort, California. In May, while camped in Missouri, Donner and his group joined members from another wagon train and formed the Donner Party, named after their elected captain. Donner predicted the journey would put everyone in sunny California by June. He and 86 fellow travelers were in for a big surprise.

Trouble on the Trail

The party had gotten as far as Fort Laramie in what is now Wyoming by the end of June, when they ran into another traveler. He was headed eastbound, having used a faster, though treacherous, route from the West through the desert, one that he did not recommend. Regardless, the Donner Party took the "shortcut," which put them three weeks behind schedule. By this time, many of the travelers had fallen ill, and most of the group's animals had either died or wandered off.

In the middle of October, the group got stuck in a monstrous mountain blizzard, still more than 100 miles from its destination.

Dwindling Supplies

The group was stranded in the Sierra Nevada mountain range for a few months. When the food supplies they had brought with them ran out, the oxen were slaughtered and eaten. Journals and letters from members of the party reveal that before very long, the only "food" available consisted of twigs, the bones of decaying animals, and boiled leather hides.

Eventually, a small faction of the Donner Party set out to find help. The rest of the party was too weak to travel, and conditions for them only worsened.

Shocking Discoveries

The rescue group, which consisted of the few members who remained, finally found help in California. Accounts of what the first relief team saw when they arrived at the camp depict group members who were starving, freezing, and delirious. Those who were able to make the recovery trip were taken at that point; the rest were forced to wait for a second rescue team.

As reported by the second group of rescuers, some of the remaining members of the Donner Party had resorted to cannibalism in order to make it through the winter. The survivors eventually reached Sutter's Fort more than a year after the party's departure from Independence, Missouri, and about six months after their expected arrival. Two-thirds of the men and one-third of the women and children had died on the journey.

The Aftermath
Not surprisingly, when word got out that settlers trapped in the mountains had eaten other human beings to stay alive, migration to California slowed for a while. When gold was discovered in 1848, images of the imperiled Donner Party were replaced by dreams of newfound wealth in the West.

Today, near the eastern shore of Donner Lake, the Donner Memorial State Park commemorates the courage and the disaster that was the Donner Party's journey. The area of nearby Alder Creek, the site of the second Donner camp, is a designated National Historic Landmark.

Q. Who invented anesthesia?

A. In the middle of the 19th century, three intoxicating solvents with bad reputations became the first crude "switches" that could turn consciousness off and on—paving the way for the revolution of painless surgical medicine.

On March 30, 1842, a doctor from rural Georgia laid an ether-soaked towel across the mouth and nose of a young patient with two cysts on the back of his neck. The physician, Crawford Williamson Long, excised one of the growths while his patient was under. In the process, he made medical and scientific history. Long was perhaps the first doctor to use what is today called a "general anesthetic"—a substance that reduces or eliminates conscious awareness in a patient, allowing a doctor to perform incisions, sutures, and all other surgical procedures in between.

The "general"—which means complete or near-complete unconsciousness—is quite different from the targeted "local" anesthetic, an invention with origins shrouded in mystery. (Some ancient Inca trepanation rituals involved drilling a hole in the patient's skull to allow evil spirits to escape; to reduce the literally mind-numbing pain, the Incan shaman chewed leaves of the narcotic coca plant and spat the paste into the subject's wound.)

Unfortunately for Georgia's Dr. Long, the awards and acclaim that should have accompanied his medical milestone went to a dentist from Boston, who used ether four years later to knock out a patient in order to remove a tooth. Because this procedure was performed at the world-renowned Massachusetts General Hospital—and not at a backwoods country practice in the Deep South—the fame of the Massachusetts innovator, William T. G. Morton, was practically assured. Within two months of Morton's tooth extraction, doctors across Europe were toasting the Yankee who had invented pain-free surgery.

The story of the stolen spotlight, however, can't entirely be blamed on the prejudice of urban versus rural or North versus South. Long, who was known to enjoy the occasional "ether frolic," didn't publicize his use of ether as a general anesthetic until 1849, seven years after his initial use of it, and three years after Morton's world-acclaimed surgery.

Wake Up, Mr. Green. Mr. Green?
By 1849, a London physician, John Snow, had invented a specialized ether inhaler to better administer a safe but effective dose of the painless surgical gas. Snow was responding to the need for more scientific care in the fledgling field of anesthesiology. Lethal doses of ether had already been administered in some botched surgeries, and Snow eventually championed chloroform, which, he would later write, is "almost impossible...[to cause] a death...in the hands of a medical man who is applying it with ordinary intelligence and attention."

Ether and chloroform each had their downsides, though. Chloroform could damage the liver and occasionally even cause cardiac arrest, but ether required more time for the patient to both enter and exit the anesthetized state.

Nothing to Laugh About
Some American practitioners championed a third popular early anesthetic: nitrous oxide, or "laughing gas," although its reputation suffered when not enough of it was administered in an early demonstration during a tooth extraction at Harvard Medical School. When the patient cried out in pain, the dentist, Horace Wells, was booed out of the room. In a turn of tragic irony, Wells later became a chloroform addict and committed suicide in 1848, just three years after the Harvard fiasco.

By the 1860s and '70s, many surgeons had given up advocating one gas over another, preferring instead to use a mixture—either chloroform or nitrous oxide to induce anesthesia, followed by ether to keep the patient in an unconscious state.

Q. How did Harvard get started?

A. The Massachusetts Bay Colony founded Harvard—which is the oldest institution of higher learning in the United States—in 1636. Today, Harvard is famed for a vast endowment, but its early days were marked by a struggle to get by.

The School's Scandalous First Leader

In 1640, the tiny college of Harvard was in crisis. Founded four years before by the Massachusetts Bay Colony, Harvard had a student body of nine, a "yard" liberated from cows, and a single, hated instructor.

Harvard's 30-year-old schoolmaster, Nathaniel Eaton, was known to beat wayward students. Other students charged Eaton's wife, Elizabeth, of putting goat dung into their cornmeal porridge, or "hasty pudding." (Harvard's theatrical society is named for the dish.) Finally, Master Eaton went too far and was hauled into court after clubbing a scholar with a walnut-tree cudgel. He was also accused of embezzling 100 pounds (then an ample sum).

In 1639, Eaton and his wife were sent packing. Master Eaton returned to England, was made a vicar, and then died in debtor's prison. Following the Eaton affair, Harvard's reputation lay in tatters; its operations were suspended, and its students were scattered.

The Roots of Learning

The money and work Massachusetts had put into the school seemed for naught. The colony's General Court had allotted 400 pounds for a college in what became known as Cambridge, Massachusetts—across the Charles River from Boston. The school was named for John Harvard, a clergyman from England's Cambridge

University, which at the time was known to be a hotbed of Puritanism, the severe, idealistic faith opposed to the dominant Church of England.

John Harvard was a scholar whose family had known William Shakespeare. When the plague felled his brothers and his father, John inherited a considerable estate, including the Queen's Head Tavern. After immigrating to the Boston region, he became a preacher in Charleston, but his career was short. In 1638, at the age of 31, he died of consumption, having bequeathed money and his personal library to the planned college.

Comeback Under the First President

In 1640, the colony's founders were desperate for educational cachet. They offered the post of Harvard president to Henry Dunster, a new arrival from England and another graduate of Cambridge University.

The energetic Dunster tapped into the colony's inherent educational edge. Many of the new Puritan arrivals had studied at the Oxford and Cambridge academies: Some 130 alumni of the two schools were in New England by 1646. Dunster himself was a leading scholar in biblical tongues such as Hebrew.

Led primarily by a Protestant culture that stressed reading the Bible, Boston set up the first free grammar school in 1635. Within 12 years, every town in Massachusetts was required by law to have one. Harvard's new president mandated a four-year graduation requirement and rode out angry students who protested over a commencement fee. Dunster obtained Harvard's charter and authored the school's "Rules and Precepts." He bankrolled the facilities through donations of livestock and, over the course of 13 years, some 250 pounds of wheat. He took a modest salary, being underpaid through 14 years of service, and piled up personal debts. Fortunately, his wife, Elizabeth

Glover, kept a printing press in their home. It was the American colonies' first press, and its profits underwrote her husband's work. Dunster managed to turn the school around. Harvard's reputation soared, and students from throughout the colonies, the Caribbean, and the mother country flocked to newly built dorms.

Religious Schisms and a President's Heresies

Dunster tripped up on one of the many religious disputes roiling the Puritan colony. In 1648, it was a criminal offense to engage in "Blasphemy, Heresie, open contempt of the Word preached, Profanation of the Lord's Day"; separation of church and state was unknown.

A source of controversy was infant baptism, which the Puritan fathers required by law. Drawing on his biblical knowledge, Dunster noted that John the Baptist had baptized the adult Jesus, but he could find no biblical examples of children being baptized.

In 1653, he refused to have his son Jonathan baptized. At Cambridge's Congregational Church, Dunster preached against "corruptions stealing into the Church, which every faithful Christian ought to [bear] witness against."

This put the Puritans of Boston and Cambridge in a quandary. Dunster's views made him a heretic, yet he was much liked for his work at the college. Early the next year, the colony's officers wrote that Dunster "hath by his practice and opinions rendered himself offensive to this government." They assembled a conference of 11 ministers and elders to interrogate him. Egged on by this assembly, in May 1654 the General Court forbade schools to employ those "that have manifested themselves unsound in the faith, or scandalous in their lives." Dunster resigned from Harvard.

The ex-president then petitioned the court to let him to stay in the colony until he could repay the many debts he'd accumulated from his work. Court authorities coldly responded that, "they did not know of [such] extraordinary labor or sacrifices. For the space of 14 years we know of none." Dunster, with Elizabeth and their youngest child ill, then beseeched the court to at least let his family stay the winter. The magistrates agreed grudgingly, but the following spring they banished the Dunster family to the backwater town of Scituate. Harvard's first president died there four years later, at the age of 47.

Q. Where was the War of Jenkins's Ear?

A. Along the border between Georgia and Florida. The Spanish were well established in Florida before the English colonized Georgia, and tension between the two countries in the area had been thick for some time. The war got its name from an incident in 1731, a year before Georgia was chartered. English Captain Robert Jenkins was accused of piracy by a Spanish officer who then lopped off his ear. The situation didn't heat up until 1740, however, when James Oglethorpe invaded Spanish Florida. He couldn't hold his territory and retreated back to Georgia, where his forces held off Spanish invasion in 1742. In the end, little was gained or lost between the two colonies.

Q. What happened to the Roanoke Island colony?

A. Twenty years before England established its first successful colony in the New World, an entire village of English colonists disappeared in what would later be known as North Carolina. Did these pioneers all perish? Did Native Americans capture them? Did they join a friendly tribe? Could they have left descendants who live among us today?

Timing Is Everything

Talk about bad timing. As far as John White was concerned, England couldn't have picked a worse time to go to war. It was November 1587, and White had just arrived in England from the New World. He intended to gather relief supplies and immediately sail back to Roanoke Island, where he had left more than 100 colonists who were running short of food. Unfortunately, the English were gearing up to fight Spain. Every seaworthy ship, including White's, was pressed into naval service. Not a one could be spared for his return voyage to America.

Nobody Home

When John White finally returned to North America three years later, he was dismayed to discover that the colonists he had left behind were nowhere to be found. Instead, he stumbled upon a mystery—one that has never been solved.

The village that White and company had founded in 1587 on Roanoke Island lay completely deserted. Houses had been dismantled (as if someone planned to move them), but the pieces lay in the long grass along with iron tools and farming equipment. A stout stockade made of logs stood empty.

White found no sign of his daughter Eleanor, her husband Ananias, or their daughter Virginia Dare—the first English child born in America. None of the 87 men, 17 women, and 11 children remained. No bodies or obvious gravesites offered clues to their fate. The only clues—if they were clues—that White could find were the letters CRO carved into a tree trunk and the word CROATOAN carved into a log of the abandoned fort.

No Forwarding Address

All White could do was hope that the colonists had been taken in by friendly natives.

Croatoan—also spelled "Croatan"—was the name of a barrier island to the south and also the name of a tribe of Native Americans that lived on that island. Unlike other area tribes, the Croatoans had been friendly to English newcomers, and one of them, Manteo, had traveled to England with earlier explorers and returned to act as interpreter for the Roanoke colony. Had the colonists, with Manteo's help, moved to Croatoan? Were they safe among friends?

White tried to find out, but his timing was rotten once again. He had arrived on the Carolina coast as a hurricane bore down on the region. The storm hit before he could mount a search. His ship was blown past Croatoan Island and out to sea. Although the ship and crew survived the storm and made it back to England, White was stuck again. He tried repeatedly but failed to raise money for another search party.

No one has ever learned the fate of the Roanoke Island colonists, but there is no shortage of theories as to what happened to them. A small sailing vessel and other boats that White had left with them were gone when he returned. It's possible that the colonists used the vessels to travel to another island or to the mainland. White had talked with others before he left about possibly moving the settlement to a more secure location inland. It's even possible that the colonists tired of waiting for White's return and tried to sail back to England. If so, they would have perished at sea. Yet there are at least a few shreds of hearsay evidence that the colonists survived in America.

Rumors of Survivors
In 1607, Captain John Smith and company established the first successful English settlement in North America at Jamestown, Virginia. The colony's secretary, William Strachey, wrote four years later about hearing a report of four English men, two boys, and one young woman who had been sighted south of Jamestown at a settlement of the Eno tribe, where they were being used as slaves. If the report was true, who else could these English have been but Roanoke survivors?

For more than a century after the colonists' disappearance, stories emerged of gray-eyed Native Americans and English-speaking villages in North Carolina and Virginia. In 1709, an English surveyor said members of the Hatteras tribe living on North Carolina's Outer Banks—some of them with light-colored eyes—claimed to be descendants of white people. It's possible that the Hatteras were the same people that the 1587 colonists called Croatoan.

In the intervening centuries, many of the individual tribes of the region have disappeared. Some died out. Others were absorbed into larger groups such as the Tuscarora. One surviving group, the Lumbee, has also been called Croatoan. The Lumbee, who still live in North Carolina, often have Caucasian features. Could they be descendants of Roanoke colonists? Many among the Lumbee dismiss the notion as fanciful, but the tribe has long been thought to be of mixed heritage and has been speaking English so long that none among them know what language preceded it.

Q. Who was known as "Lady Lindy"?

A. Amelia Earhart. America's most famous female aviator, Earhart was dubbed "Lady Lindy" (after aviator Charles Lindbergh) for her many accomplishments in the air. During the 1920s and '30s, Earhart set altitude and speed records and championed the place of women in the nascent field of aviation. Her brilliant career was cut short when she disappeared during an attempt to fly around the world in 1937.

Q. When was the Comstock Lode discovered, and what was the significance of this new find?

A. The Comstock Lode was discovered in the spring of 1859. It was the first major silver discovery in the United States, and the silver that was mined helped fund the Union during the Civil War.

Q. King Philip's War may have been early America's worst conflict. Where was it fought?

A. In Massachusetts and Rhode Island. King Philip was also known as Metacom, and he was the son of Massasoit, the Wampanoag leader who had saved the original Plymouth colony by helping the Pilgrims establish themselves and teaching them to farm in the New World. By 1675, the population of English colonists in New England had grown to about 52,000, and Metacom feared that colonists would force the Wampanoag off their traditional lands. Relations between Native Americans and English colonists became more and more tense, and for 14 months in 1675 and '76, both sides set modern Massachusetts and Rhode Island aflame, destroying towns, villages, and property. In August 1676, however, Plymouth militia and Native American allies tracked Metacom down at Mount Hope, Rhode Island, where they beheaded, drew, and quartered him, to end the hostilities.

Q. What did Nellie Bly find on Blackwell's Island?

A. If you visit Roosevelt Island, you'll notice a building called the Octagon. These days, it's a posh condominium, but it was once the site of human injustice and chaos, 19th-century-style. Crackerjack reporter—and beloved New Yorker—Nellie Bly uncovered the story.

A little slip of land in the East River, Roosevelt Island was called Blackwell's Island during the 18th and 19th centuries. It was just farmland and hunting ground initially, but a prison was built in 1832, and several years later, it was joined by the New York Lunatic Asylum, which was dominated by the Octagon Tower. The structure was beautiful, with an enormous spiral staircase and a domed, octagonal roof. But from the start, the asylum was grossly mismanaged. More than 1,700 mentally ill inmates were crammed inside (twice as many as should have been there), and although nurses were on duty, inmates from the nearby prison handled most of the supervision.

Over the next few decades, more prisons, asylums, and workhouses were built on Blackwell's, helping to inspire the island's new nickname—Welfare Island. Mortality was high because the care was so poor. Infants born there rarely lived to see adolescence. Any time spent on Blackwell's Island was too long for most.

The Girl's Got Sass

Help was on the way. Born in Pennsylvania in 1864, Elizabeth Jane Cochrane was a spitfire from the start. As a teen, she wrote an angry editorial to the *Pittsburgh Dispatch* about an article she found insulting to women. The editor was so impressed he hired her. Elizabeth assumed the pen name "Nellie Bly" (after a popular song) and lobbied hard for juicy stories. Although she landed a few, newspaperwomen at that time were relegated to the fashion and arts beats, a fate Bly fought against. Yearning for more substantive work, she left the *Dispatch* for New York City in 1887. She had bigger fish to fry.

Bly got a job at Joseph Pulitzer's *New York World* in hopes of significant stories. She already had one to pitch—she would feign insanity and get into the Women's Lunatic Asylum on Blackwell's Island. Everyone had heard about the dastardly conditions there, but no one had dared check it out. Bly's editors were duly impressed and gave their new employee the green light.

That night, Nellie checked into a Manhattan boardinghouse and commenced to freak everyone out. She acted bizarrely, dirtied her face, and feigned amnesia. Before long, the police came and took her away—straight into the heart of Blackwell's insane asylum.

From Bad to Worse

What the 23-year-old reporter found when she got there was worse than she had feared. For the next ten days, she endured the terrors and neglect that long-term inmates knew all too well. Life in the asylum was reduced to the animal level. Rotten meat and thin broth, along with lumps of nearly inedible dough, were all inmates were given to eat. And to wash it all down? Unclean drinking water.

Everyone was dirty, surrounded by their own filth and excrement from the rats that had free reign over the place. Baths consisted of buckets of ice water poured over the head, and the residents passed their days on cold, hard benches in stultifying boredom.

Bly's editors rescued her after ten days, and Nellie wrote her exposé, called *Ten Days in a Mad-House*. The story blew up in the faces of the tin gods who controlled the prison and the asylum. Physicians and staff members tried to do damage control, but it was no use. A grand jury investigation commenced, and before long, new standards—many of which were suggested by Nellie herself—were implemented in institutions statewide. Moneys were allocated, and the asylum on Blackwell's received long overdue repair and rehabilitation.

As for the young reporter, she'd never have to go back to the fashion pages again. Bly continued to seek out adventure and remained a respected investigative reporter until she retired in 1895. Celebrated after that as an industrialist, Nellie remained in New York City until her death in 1922.

Law and Order

Q. When was the first FBI's Most Wanted list published?

A. 1950. In late 1949, J. Edgar Hoover of the FBI and William Kinsey Hutchinson of the International News Service (forerunner of United Press International) decided to partner up to catch America's most wanted fugitives. After the first published Most Wanted list received a great deal of attention, the FBI decided to make releasing the list a regular practice. With the Most Wanted list, the FBI came to rely on the vigilance of good citizens for its most dangerous work.

When the list first appeared in 1950, it included bank robbers and car thieves, but over time, the nature of the criminals who made the list changed. The 1970s saw a focus on organized crime figures. More recently, emphasis has shifted to terrorists and drug dealers.

Over the years, the program has proved remarkably effective. Nearly 500 criminals have appeared on the list, and more than 90 percent of them have been captured. About a third of these former fugitives were caught as a direct result of tips from the public.

Q. Who makes the cut on the FBI's Most Wanted list?

A. Criminals must meet two criteria in order to become candidates for the world's most famous rogues gallery. First, they must have an extensive record of serious criminal activity or a recent criminal history that poses a particular threat to public safety. Second, there must be a reasonable likelihood that publicity from their presence on the list will aid in their capture. Criminals are only removed from the list for three reasons—they are captured, the charges against them are dropped, or they no longer fit the criteria for the list.

Q. What conspirators helped Booth kill President Lincoln?

A. John Wilkes Booth is well known for his assassination of President Abraham Lincoln at Ford's Theatre on April 14, 1865, but the rather lengthy list of his coconspirators has not been quite so memorable.

A popular Shakespearean stage actor who traveled the country performing, John Wilkes Booth could have kept busy enjoying his notoriety and fame. Instead, inspired by the secession of the Southern states that set off the Civil War, he was firmly entrenched in his racist beliefs and loyalty to the Confederacy. Once Lincoln freed the slaves in the rebelling states, a conviction took hold in Booth's mind, branding the abolitionist president as his archenemy. Dead set on bringing down Lincoln and preserving the Confederacy and the institution of slavery, Booth began to plot his attack. Initially, he planned to kidnap Lincoln and then ransom him for captive Confederate soldiers, but the conspiracy evolved, of course, into the first presidential assassination in U.S. history.

The Accomplices

Booth, who was charismatic and persuasive, had no trouble forming a gang of like-minded conspirators. Samuel Arnold, George Atzerodt, David Herold, Lewis Powell, John Surratt, and Michael O'Laughlen all joined with Booth to design various plots that would achieve victory for the South and cause trouble for Lincoln and his backers.

Meeting regularly at a boardinghouse run by Mary Surratt, the mother of one of the conspirators, the club decided to kidnap Lincoln in early 1865. They would simply snatch him from his box at a play and then ransom him for a few imprisoned Confederate soldiers. It would be a twofold victory, as they would cause grievance for their nemesis and bring the Confederacy closer to victory. Their plan was thwarted, though, when Lincoln failed to appear at the scheduled event. Similar plans were hatched, but for various reasons, none of the kidnapping plots came to fruition. Frustrated with his inability to capture Lincoln and spurred by Lincoln's continued attempts to dismantle the system of slavery, Booth determined that kidnapping was simply not enough: Lincoln must die!

Arnold, John Surratt, and O'Laughlen later swore that they knew nothing of the plot to commit murder, but Atzerodt, Herold, and Powell most certainly did. They each had their own assigned roles in the grand assassination plot, unsuccessful though they were in carrying out those parts. Atzerodt was slated to assassinate Vice President Andrew Johnson, while Powell and Herold were scheduled to kill Secretary of State William Seward. All three assassinations were planned for the same time on the evening of April 14.

Going into Action

Only Booth found complete success in the mission, however. Atzerodt apparently backed down from his assignment in fear. Powell cut a path of carnage through the Seward mansion, stabbing the secretary of state in the face and neck and wounding two of Seward's sons, a daughter, a soldier guarding Seward, and a messenger, although no one was killed. Herold had been with Powell but ran away when the mission didn't seem to be going smoothly. Booth shot Lincoln in the back of the head. The president died on the morning of April 15.

Booth immediately fled the scene, injuring a leg in his mad dash. He met up with Herold, and the pair was on the run for two weeks before finally being discovered on a small farm. The fugitives were holed up in a barn—Herold surrendered, but when Booth refused to do the same, soldiers set the barn on fire. In the ensuing melee, Booth was shot in the neck; he died a few hours later. Atzerodt, Herold, and Powell were hanged for their crimes, as was one more purported coconspirator, Mary Surratt. She ran the boardinghouse in which much of this plot was hatched, a plot that definitely included her son at various times. Her specific involvement and knowledge of the affair, however, has frequently been challenged.

The rest of the original coconspirators, as well as others with suspicious acquaintance to the group, were sentenced to jail time for their involvement.

Q. How did Prohibition get started?

A. Sure, Prohibition didn't work, but a study of its roots shows why people thought an alcohol ban was feasible enough.

But First . . .
Did you bring your ax? Let's shatter a kegful of mythology!
Did you know that . . .

. . . the Prohibition movement actually began before the
Civil War? The temperance movement registered local
victories as early as the 1850s.

. . . one-third of the federal budget ran on ethanol? This
was before federal income tax became the main source
of revenue.

. . . Prohibition didn't ban alcohol consumption? Clubs
that stocked up on liquor before Prohibition legally served
it throughout.

. . . women's suffrage didn't affect the passage of
Prohibition? The Eighteenth Amendment enacted
Prohibition. The Nineteenth Amendment gave women
the vote.

. . . Prohibition didn't create gangs? The gangs were
already there. They just took advantage of a golden
opportunity.

. . . Eliot Ness's "Untouchables" really existed? They were
agents of the Bureau of Prohibition.

Temperance
Strictly speaking, *temperance* means moderation, not
abstinence. By the early 1800s, most people realized that
drunkenness wasn't particularly healthy. As the industrial
age gathered steam, working while intoxicated went from
"bad behavior" to "asking for an industrial maiming by
enormous machinery." Immigration also factored, for
nativist sentiment ran high in the 1800s. Many Americans
didn't like immigrants with foreign accents (many of
whom saw nothing wrong with tying one on) and made
alcohol an "us versus them" issue.

The XX (Chromosome) Factor
Women, logically, formed the backbone of the temperance
movement. Just because you can't vote doesn't mean

your brain is disconnected. With a woman's social role limited to home and family, whatever disabled the home's primary wage-earner threatened home economics. Worse still, alcohol abuse has always gone fist-in-mouth with domestic violence.

Organizations and Advances
In 1869, the Prohibition Party was formed to run antialcohol candidates. It typically polled 200,000+ popular presidential votes from 1888 to 1920 but never greatly influenced national politics in and of itself. The compressed political energy and intellect of American women—denied access to congressional seats and judgeships—found its outlet in 1873: the Woman's Christian Temperance Union (WCTU), which still exists today. By 1890, the WCTU counted 150,000 members.

Meanwhile, the male-dominated Anti-Saloon League (ASL) was founded in 1893 and achieved rapid successes due to smart campaigning. By appealing to churches and campaigning against Demon Rum's local bad guys, it drew in nonprohibitionists who disapproved of the entire saloon/bar/tavern culture. While the ASL would later hog the credit for the Eighteenth Amendment, the WCTU laid the foundation for credible temperance activism.

Only three states were "dry" before 1893. In 1913, the ASL began advocating Prohibition via constitutional amendment. By 1914, there were 14 dry states, encompassing nearly half the population. By 1917, another 12 had dried up. In that same year, the Supreme Court ruled that Americans didn't have a constitutional right to keep alcohol at home. Prohibition's ax, long in forging, now had a sturdy handle.

Eighteenth Amendment
By January 29, 1919, the necessary 36 states had ratified this amendment. In October of that year, Congress

passed the Volstead Act to enforce the amendment. One year later, it would be illegal to manufacture, sell, or transport intoxicating liquors. Of course, everyone stopped drinking.

Okay, that's enough laughter. What we got was the Roaring Twenties. Alcohol went underground, corrupting police departments and providing limitless opportunity for lawbreakers. The understaffed, oft-bought-and-paid-for Bureau of Prohibition couldn't possibly keep up. America's War on Alcohol worked no better than the later War on Drugs, which would so casually ignore history's lessons.

Enough Already
On December 5, 1933, the Twenty-first Amendment repealed the Eighteenth—the only such repeal in U.S. history. Prohibition was over. Everyone had a few beers, and then got busy worrying about marijuana.

Q. On what date did federal agents raid the Mount Carmel Center near Waco, Texas, starting a gunfight that ultimately set up a 51-day siege of the Branch Davidian compound?

A. February 28, 1993. The FBI approached the Branch Davidian compound after reports surfaced about illegal firearms at the compound. As they attempted to serve the warrant and begin their search, shots rang out. The agents maintain that the Branch Davidians fired the first shots, while the Branch Davidians claim that they did not fire until first fired upon. Regardless, a standoff ensued that lasted 51 days. On April 19, 1993, federal agents, in an attempt to force the Davidians out, launched tear gas into the compound. Leader David Koresh and the Davidians began shooting. About six hours after the gassing began, fires erupted inside the compound. (Accusations were made as to which side was responsible for the fires, but later investigations concluded that the Branch Davidians had set the fires.) Shots continued to ring out, and agents on the scene reportedly believed the Davidians were either killing themselves or shooting one another. Firefighters came to the scene but were not allowed to combat the flames for some time out of fear for their safety in the midst of the gunfire. After the smoke cleared, more than 80 people were dead, including 17 children. Koresh was identified by dental records; he had been killed by a gunshot to the head.

Q. What American building was bombed on April 19, 1995?

A. The Alfred P. Murrah Federal Building in downtown Oklahoma City. The bombing killed 168 people (including 19 children in the building's day-care center) and injured more than 500 others. Timothy McVeigh and Terry Nichols were both charged and arrested. McVeigh, a homegrown American terrorist, had parked a rented Ryder truck in front of the building and detonated a bomb shortly after 9:00 A.M. McVeigh was executed on June 11, 2001, and Terry Nichols is serving a life sentence.

Q. What are some of America's coldest cases?

A. They were gruesome crimes that shocked us with their brutality. But as time passed, we heard less and less about them until we forgot about the crime, not even realizing that the perpetrator remained among us. Yet the files remain open, and the families of the victims live on in a state of semi-paralysis. Here are some of America's most famous cold cases.

Elizabeth Short

Elizabeth Short, also known as the Black Dahlia, was murdered in 1947. Like thousands of others, Elizabeth wanted to be a star. Unlike the bevy of blondes who trekked to Hollywood, this 22-year-old beauty from Massachusetts was dark and mysterious. She was last seen alive outside the Biltmore Hotel in Los Angeles on the evening of January 9, 1947.

Short's body was found on a vacant lot in Los Angeles. It had been cut in half at the waist and both parts had been drained of blood and then cleaned. Her body parts appeared to be surgically dissected, and her remains were suggestively posed. Despite receiving a number of false confessions and taunting letters that admonished police to "catch me if you can," the crime remains unsolved.

The Zodiac Killer

The Zodiac Killer was responsible for several murders in the San Francisco area in the 1960s and 1970s. His victims were shot, stabbed, and bludgeoned to death. After the first few kills, he began sending letters to the local press in which he taunted police and made public threats, such as planning to blow up a school bus. In a letter sent to the *San Francisco Chronicle* two days after the murder of cabbie Paul Stine in October 1969, the killer, who called himself "The Zodiac," included in the package pieces of Stine's blood-soaked shirt. In the letters, which continued until 1978, he claimed a cumulative tally of 37 murders.

The Torso Killer

In Cleveland, Ohio, during the 1930s, more than a dozen limbless torsos were found. Despite the efforts of famed crime fighter Eliot Ness, the torso killer was never found. The first two bodies, found in September 1935, were missing heads and had been horribly mutilated. Similar murders occurred during the next three years. Desperate to stop the killings, Ness ordered a raid on a run-down area known as Kingsbury's Run, where most of the victims were from. The place was torched, and hundreds of vagrants were taken into custody. After that, there were no more killings.

The key suspect in the murders was Frank Dolezal, a vagrant who lived in the area. He was a known bully with a fiery temper. Dolezal was arrested and subsequently confessed, but his confession was full of inaccuracies. He died shortly thereafter under suspicious circumstances.

Bob Crane
In 1978, Bob Crane, star of TV's *Hogan's Heroes*, was clubbed to death in his apartment. Crane shared a close friendship with John Carpenter, a pioneer in the development of video technology. The two shared an affinity for debauchery and sexual excesses, which were recorded on videotape. But by late 1978, Crane was tiring of Carpenter's dependence on him and had let him know that the friendship was over.

The following day, June 29, 1978, Crane was bludgeoned to death with a camera tripod in his Scottsdale, Arizona, apartment. Suspicion immediately fell on Carpenter, and a small spattering of blood was found in Carpenter's rental car, but police were unable to connect it to the crime. Examiners also found a tiny piece of human tissue in the car. Sixteen years after the killing, Carpenter finally went to trial, but he was acquitted due to lack of evidence.

Jimmy Hoffa
In 1975, labor leader Jimmy Hoffa disappeared on his way to a Detroit-area restaurant. Hoffa was the president

of the Teamsters Union during the 1950s and 1960s. In 1964, he went to jail for bribing a grand juror investigating corruption in the union. In 1971, he was released on the condition that he not participate in any further union activity. Hoffa was preparing a legal challenge to that injunction when he disappeared on July 30, 1975. He was last seen in the parking lot of the Machus Red Fox Restaurant.

Hoffa had strong connections to the Mafia, and several mobsters have claimed that he met a grisly end on their say so. Although his body has never been found, authorities officially declared him dead on July 30, 1982. As recently as November 2006, the FBI dug up farmland in Michigan hoping to turn up a corpse. So far, no luck.

JonBenét Ramsey
In the early hours of December 26, 1996, Patsy Ramsey reported that her six-year-old daughter, JonBenét, had been abducted from her Boulder, Colorado, home. Police rushed to the Ramsey home where, hours later, John Ramsey found his little girl dead in the basement. She had been battered, sexually assaulted, and strangled.

Police found several tantalizing bits of evidence—a number of footprints, a rope that did not belong on the premises, marks on the body that suggested the use of a stun gun, and DNA samples on the girl's body. The ransom note was also suspicious. Police found that it was written with a pen and pad of paper belonging to the Ramseys. The amount demanded, $118,000, was a surprisingly small amount, considering that John Ramsey was worth more than $6 million. It is also interesting to note that Mr. Ramsey had just received a year-end bonus of $118,117.50.

A number of suspects were considered, but one by one, they were cleared. Finally, the police zeroed in on the parents. For years, the Ramseys were put under intense pressure by authorities and the public alike to confess to the murder. However, a grand jury investigation ended with no indictments. In 2003, a judge ruled that an intruder had killed JonBenét. Then, in August 2006, John Mark Karr confessed, claiming that he was with the girl when she died. However, Karr's DNA did not match that found on JonBenét. He was not charged, and the case remains unsolved.

Q. **Who was the only American executed for desertion during World War II?**

A. Eddie Slovik. Shortly after arriving in Europe, Slovik became involved in the fighting around the Hurtgen Forest, where the Allies suffered 33,000 casualties. Eddie was terrified, and after submitting numerous requests to be removed from the front lines, he deserted. He turned himself in to authorities the next day and was imprisoned in Belgium, tried by a court-martial committee, found guilty, and sentenced to death. Many men had been sentenced to death for desertion since the war began, but the United States had not executed one of its own soldiers since the Civil War. Eddie and most others involved with the case assumed he would stay in jail until the end of the war. Army authorities opted to carry out Slovik's sentence, however. Eddie wrote to General Dwight D. Eisenhower begging for clemency, but Eisenhower refused to rescind the order. On January 31, 1945, Private Eddie Slovik was executed by a 12-man firing squad.

Q. What did Lizzie Borden do?

A. Despite the famous playground verse that leaves little doubt about her guilt, Lizzie Borden was never convicted of murdering her father and stepmother.

It was a sensational crime that captured the public imagination of late-19th-century America. On the morning of August 4, 1892, in Fall River, Massachusetts, the bodies of Andrew Borden and his second wife, Abby, were found slaughtered in the home they shared with an Irish maid and Andrew's 32-year-old daughter, Lizzie. A second daughter, Emma, was away from home at the time.

Rumors and Rhyme
Although Lizzie was a devout, church-going Sunday school teacher, she was charged with the horrific murders and was immortalized in this popular rhyme: "Lizzie Borden took an ax and gave her mother 40 whacks. When she saw what she had done, she gave her father 41." In reality, her stepmother was struck 19 times, killed in an upstairs bedroom with the same ax that crushed her husband's skull while he slept on a couch downstairs. In that gruesome attack, his face took 11 blows, one of which cut his eye in two and another that severed his nose.

Andrew was one of the wealthiest men in Fall River. By reputation, he was also one of the meanest. The prosecution alleged that Lizzie's motivation for the murders was financial—she had hoped to inherit her father's estate. Despite the large quantity of blood at the crime scene, the police were unable to find any blood-soaked clothing worn by Lizzie when she allegedly committed the crimes.

Ultimately Innocent
Lizzie's defense counsel successfully had their client's contradictory inquest testimony ruled inadmissible, along

with all evidence relating to her earlier attempts to purchase poison from a local drugstore. On June 19, 1893, the jury in the case returned its verdict of not guilty.

Q. What was the CIA research project MKULTRA?

A. From the mid-1950s through at least the early 1970s, thousands of unwitting Americans and Canadians became part of a bizarre CIA research project codenamed MKULTRA. Participants were secretly "brainwashed"—drugged with LSD and other hallucinogens, subjected to electro-convulsive shock therapy, and manipulated with abusive mind-control techniques.

MKULTRA began in 1953 under the orders of CIA director Allen Dulles. The program, which was in direct violation of the human rights provisions of the Nuremberg Code that the United States helped establish after World War II, was developed in response to reports that U.S. prisoners of war in Korea were being subjected to Communist mind-control techniques.

CIA researchers hoped to find a "truth drug" that could be used on Soviet agents, as well as drugs that could be used against foreign leaders (one documented scheme involved an attempt in 1960 to dose Fidel Castro with LSD). They also aimed to develop means of mind control that would benefit U.S. intelligence, perhaps including the creation of so-called "Manchurian Candidates" to carry out assassinations. As part of MKULTRA, the CIA investigated parapsychology and such phenomena as hypnosis, telepathy, precognition, photokinesis, and "remote viewing."

MKULTRA was headed by Dr. Sidney Gottlieb, a military psychiatrist and chemist known as the "Black Sorcerer," who specialized in concocting deadly poisons. More than 30 universities and scientific institutes took part in MKULTRA. LSD and other mind-altering drugs including heroin, mescaline, psilocybin, scopolamine, marijuana, and sodium pentothal were given to CIA employees, military personnel, and other government workers, often without the subjects' knowledge or prior consent. To broaden their subject pool, researchers targeted unsuspecting civilians, often those in vulnerable or socially compromising situations. Prison inmates, prostitutes, and mentally ill hospital patients were often used. In a project codenamed Operation Midnight Climax, the CIA set up brothels in several U.S. cities to lure men as unwitting test subjects. Rooms were equipped with cameras that filmed the experiments behind one-way mirrors. Some civilian subjects who consented to participation were used for more extreme experimentation. One group of volunteers in Kentucky was given LSD for more than 70 days straight.

LSD

In the 1960s, Dr. Gottlieb also traveled to Vietnam and conducted mind-control experiments on Viet Cong prisoners of war being held by U.S. forces. During the same time period, an unknown number of Soviet agents died in U.S. custody in Europe after being given dual intravenous injections of barbiturates and amphetamine in the CIA's search for a truth serum.

MKULTRA experiments were also carried out in Montreal, Canada, between 1957 and 1964 by Dr. Donald Ewen Cameron, a researcher in Albany, New York, who also served as president of the World Psychiatric Association and the American and Canadian psychiatric associations.

The CIA appears to have given him potentially deadly experiments to carry out at Canadian mental health institutes so U.S. citizens would not be involved. Cameron also experimented with paralytic drugs—in some cases inducing a coma in subjects for up to three months—as well as using electro-convulsive therapy at 30 times the normal voltage. The subjects were often women being treated for anxiety disorders and postpartum depression. Many suffered permanent damage. A lawsuit by victims of the experiments later uncovered that the Canadian government had also funded the project.

At least one American subject died in the experiments. Frank Olson, a U.S. army biological weapons researcher, was secretly given LSD in 1953. A week later, he fell from a hotel window in New York City following a severe psychotic episode. A CIA doctor assigned to monitor Olson claimed he jumped from the window, but an autopsy performed on Olson's exhumed remains in 1994 found that he had been knocked unconscious before the fall.

The U.S. army also conducted experiments with psycho-active drugs. A later investigation determined that nearly all army experiments involved soldiers and civilians who had given their informed consent, and that army researchers had largely followed scientific and safety protocols. Ken Kesey, who would later write *One Flew Over the Cuckoo's Nest* and become one of the originators of the hippie movement, volunteered for LSD studies at an army research center in San Francisco in 1960. LSD stolen from the army lab by test subjects was some of the first in the world used "recreationally" by civilians. The army's high ethical standards, however, seem to have been absent in at least one case. Harold Blauer, a professional tennis player in New York City who was hospitalized for depression following his divorce, died from apparent cardiac arrest during an army experiment in 1952. Blauer had been secretly injected with massive doses of mescaline.

CIA researchers eventually concluded that the effects of LSD were too unpredictable to be useful, and the agency later acknowledged that their experiments made little scientific sense. Records on 150 MKULTRA research projects were destroyed in 1973 by order of CIA Director Richard Helms. A year later, the *New York Times* first reported about CIA experiments on U.S. citizens. In 1975, congressional hearings and a report by the Rockefeller Commission revealed details of the program. In 1976, President Gerald Ford issued an executive order prohibiting experimentation with drugs on human subjects without their informed consent. Ford and CIA Director William Colby also publicly apologized to Frank Olson's family, who received $750,000 by a special act of Congress.

Though no evidence exists that the CIA succeeded in its quest to find mind-control techniques, some conspiracy theories claim that the MKULTRA project was linked to the assassination of Robert F. Kennedy. Some have argued that Kennedy's assassin, Sirhan B. Sirhan, had been subjected to mind control. Sirhan claims that he has no recollection of shooting Kennedy, despite attempts by both government prosecutors and his defense lawyers to use hypnosis to recover his memories.

Q. What is the point of multiple life sentences?

A. No, the justice system isn't secretly Buddhist. There are good reasons for multiple life sentences, and they don't have anything to do with reincarnation.

Logically enough, judges hand down multiple sentences in order to punish multiple criminal offenses. Multiple charges may be decided in the same trial, but they are still considered separate crimes and often yield separate punishments. Even in cases of life imprisonment, multiple sentences can end up being very important in the rare instances in which convictions are overturned on appeals.

Let's say a jury finds a man guilty of killing five people. The judge might sentence him to five life sentences to address the five charges. Even if any one of the convictions is overturned (or even if four of them are overturned), the murderer still has to serve a life sentence. To walk free, he would have to be exonerated of all five murders.

Furthermore, "life" doesn't always mean an entire lifetime. Depending on the sentencing guidelines of the state, the judge may sentence a person to life imprisonment with the possibility of parole. In this instance, life is the maximum length of the sentence, meaning that the defendant could conceivably go free if a parole board releases him after he's served the minimum time (thirty years, for example).

If, however, a defendant is convicted on multiple charges, the judge may hand down multiple life sentences with the possibility of parole—but the judge can also specify that those sentences be served consecutively rather than concurrently. This way, the prisoner will not get a parole hearing until the minimum time for all the sentences put together has been served.

Consider multiple life sentences to be a safeguard, a way to ensure that the bad guys never see the light of day.

Q. What happened to D. B. Cooper?

A. On the day before Thanksgiving, 1971, in Portland, Oregon, a man in his mid-forties who called himself Dan Cooper (news reports would later misidentify him as "D. B.") boarded a Northwest Orient Airlines 727 that was bound for Seattle. Dressed in a suit and tie and carrying a briefcase, Cooper was calm and polite when he handed a note to a flight attendant. The note said that his briefcase contained a bomb; he was hijacking the plane. Cooper told the crew that upon landing in Seattle, he wanted four parachutes and two hundred thousand dollars in twenty-dollar bills.

His demands were met, and Cooper released the other passengers. He ordered the pilots to fly to Mexico, but he gave specific instructions to keep the plane under ten thousand feet with the wing flaps at fifteen degrees, restricting the aircraft's speed. That night, in a cold rainstorm somewhere over southwest Washington, Cooper donned the parachutes, and with the money packed in knapsacks that were tied to his body, he jumped from the 727's rear stairs.

For several months afterward, the FBI conducted an extensive manhunt of the rugged forest terrain, but the agents were unable to find even a shred of evidence. In 1972, a copycat hijacker named Richard McCoy successfully jumped from a flight over Utah with five hundred thousand dollars and was arrested days later. At first the FBI thought McCoy was Cooper, but he didn't match the description provided by the crew of Cooper's flight. Other suspects surfaced over the years, including a Florida antiques dealer with a shady past who confessed to his wife on his deathbed that he was Cooper—though he was later discredited by DNA testing.

Cooper hadn't hurt anybody, and he had no apparent political agenda. He became a folk hero of sorts—he was immortalized in books, in song, in television documentaries, and in a movie, *The Pursuit of D. B. Cooper*. In 1980, solid evidence surfaced. An eight-year-old boy found $5,800 in rotting twenty-dollar bills along the Columbia River, and the serial numbers matched those on the cash that was given to Cooper. But while thousands of leads have been investigated over the years, the case remains the only unsolved hijacking in U.S. history.

Q. Why do cops say you have the right to remain silent?

A. It's all because of this guy named Ernesto Miranda, who took his case to the U.S. Supreme Court. In the landmark case, the Court decided that police must thoroughly inform arrested individuals of their rights, including the right to remain silent, the right to a lawyer, and an explanation that anything said to officials could be used against him or her at trial. Here's how the law that became an integral part of all arrests came to pass.

You Have the Right to Remain Silent

In 1963, following his arrest for the kidnapping and rape of an 18-year-old woman, Ernesto Miranda was arrested and placed in a Phoenix, Arizona, police lineup. When he stepped down from the gallery of suspects, Miranda asked the officers about the charges against him. His police captors implied that he had been positively identified as the kidnapper and rapist of a young woman. After two hours of interrogation, Miranda confessed.

Miranda signed a confession that included a typed paragraph indicating that his statement had been voluntary and that he had been fully aware of his legal rights.

But there was one problem—at no time during his interrogation had Miranda actually been advised of his rights. The wheels of justice had been set in motion on a highly unbalanced axle.

Anything You Say Can and Will Be Used Against You in a Court of Law

When appealing Miranda's conviction, his attorney attempted to have the confession thrown out on the grounds that his client hadn't been advised of his rights. The motion was overruled. Eventually, Miranda would be convicted on both rape and kidnapping charges and sentenced to 20 to 30 years in prison. It seemed like the end of the road for Miranda—but it was just the beginning.

You Have the Right to an Attorney

Miranda requested that the U.S. Supreme Court hear his case. His attorney, John J. Flynn, submitted a 2,000-word petition for a writ of *certiorari* (judicial review), arguing that Miranda's Fifth Amendment rights had been violated. In November 1965, the Supreme Court agreed to hear Miranda's case.

A Law Is Born

After much debate among Miranda's attorneys and the state, a decision in Miranda's favor was rendered. Chief Justice Earl Warren wrote in his *Miranda v. Arizona* opinion, "The person in custody must, prior to interrogation, be clearly informed that he has the right to remain silent, and that anything he says will be used against him in court; he must be clearly informed that he has the right to consult with a lawyer and to have the lawyer with him during interrogation, and that, if he is indigent, a lawyer will be appointed to represent him." These rights became known as Miranda Rights, and all law enforcement officials are required to recite them when they make an arrest.

Aftermath

In the wake of the U.S. Supreme Court's ruling, police departments across the nation began to issue the "Miranda warning." As for Miranda himself, his freedom was short-lived. He would be sentenced to 11 years in prison at a second trial that did not include his prior confession as evidence. Miranda was released in 1972, and he bounced in and out of jail over the next few years. On January 31, 1976, Miranda was stabbed to death in a Phoenix bar. The suspect received his Miranda warning, opted to remain silent, and due to insufficient evidence, he would not be prosecuted for Ernesto Miranda's murder.

Q. If the cops break down your door, do they have to pay for it?

A. It's not unprecedented. But don't expect any of those polite officers to take time out to write you a check while they're barreling through your house. You're going to need to hire a lawyer.

Generally speaking, in cases that involve the police causing damage to private property, they're covered by a couple of legal precepts known as governmental tort immunity and sovereign immunity. Tort immunity exempts the government from having to pay for damages. (It also allows the government to get away with a bunch of other stuff, but that's another story.) Sovereign immunity lets the government decide whether you can sue the government. You can probably guess what the government usually decides.

Let's say you are allowed to sue. You need to prove that the cops were being negligent when they broke down your door. And history has shown (to the relief of taxpayers everywhere) that in cases of simple property damage, it's fairly rare for a court to find that police were negligent. Even if the cops break down your door and then realize they've made a mistake and really meant to break down your neighbor's door, that's still considered a reasonable execution of their duties.

What constitutes negligence? One example would be an officer who breaks down your door without a warrant and without a pressing need to get in immediately. If you're "lucky" enough to have that happen, well, you may be the winner of a government-subsidized shopping spree in the door department at Home Depot.

In recent years, some state and local governments have moved to scale back governmental tort immunity. But even in those places, the people who benefit from government settlements tend to be the people who suffered most—those who were injured or had relatives who were killed or were subject to extreme violations of their civil rights. When it comes to busted doors, the government still probably won't show you a whole lot of sympathy.

Q. The controversial trial of two Italian American immigrants, Nicola Sacco and Bartolomeo Vanzetti, resulted in their execution on what date?

A. August 23, 1927. Sacco and Vanzetti were alleged anarchists who were accused of murdering two men during an armed robbery in 1920. They were arrested because they were both carrying guns at the time of the murder, though both men had alibis. Many believe their convictions were a result of prejudice against Italian American immigrants and distain for their extremist beliefs.

Q. When did the FBI open its first crime lab?

A. 1932. The FBI opened its first crime lab in Washington, D.C., with a single employee, agent Charles Appel, who focused on handwriting analysis and analyzing evidence collected from crime scenes.

Q. Whose kidnapping in 1932 led to sensational headlines around the globe?

A. Charles Lindbergh III, son of aviator Charles Lindbergh. Though the Lindberghs fulfilled the demands of the ransom note, the boy was tragically found dead 11 days after the kidnapping. German immigrant Bruno Hauptmann was apprehended after using some of the marked ransom money. He was convicted and later executed.

Q. Julius and Ethel Rosenburg were the only American citizens to be executed for espionage during the Cold War. When were they executed?

A. June 19, 1953. The Rosenbergs, accused of passing information regarding atomic weapons to the Soviet Union, were convicted of conspiracy to commit espionage during a time of war. They were executed in the electric chair at Sing Sing Correctional Facility. Both maintained their innocence until their deaths. Most historians believe Julius Rosenberg was, indeed, a spy, but his wife was likely innocent. The Rosenbergs left behind two young sons, who were eventually adopted by writer Abel Meeropol and his wife, Anne.

Q. What are blue laws?

A. Folks older than 50 probably know that blue laws are legal restrictions about doing business on Sundays. Back in the good old days, all but eight states had laws on the books that forced stores that sold nonessential items—everything except groceries and medicine—to remain closed on Sundays. By 2008, all but fifteen states had removed those statutes, and the holdouts left the issue up to their counties and cities to decide.

The idea behind the laws was that Sunday is the Sabbath and, therefore, should be a day of rest. In colonial times, blue laws reflected the common view of how decent, God-fearing people should behave and encouraged church attendance. Some of today's "Sunday" laws are more targeted: For example, Michigan doesn't allow car sales on Sundays, and several states prohibit the sale of alcohol.

A broader definition of blue laws is any anachronistic rule that enforces one group's idea of morality on the population. Laws against blasphemy, public displays of affection, adultery, and sodomy are examples of these. In the 17th century, even wearing lacy sleeves could be enough to get a man locked up in the stockade. Once, a certain Captain Kemble returned to Boston after three years at sea and kissed his wife in front of other people. He was convicted of "lewd and unseemly behavior."

Why are these rules called blue laws? A man named Reverend Samuel Peters made fun of New Haven Colony's "blue laws" in a book called *A General History of Connecticut*, published in 1781—he gets credit for first using the term. Maybe it's because the first such laws were printed on blue paper or bound in blue—no one is really sure. It may just be that these laws made people unhappy, so the word "blue" was attached to them.

Science and Nature

Q. What 1969 fire helped ignite the environmental movement?

A. The Cuyahoga River fire in 1969. Though river fires were surprisingly common in the United States in the 20th century, this one caught the nation's attention because it occurred just as the environmental movement was gaining momentum. The fire started as a train was making its way across a railroad bridge over the river in downtown Cleveland. A spark from a broken wheel touched off an explosion in a pool of volatile sludge in the water below. To make matters worse, logs, railroad ties, and other debris tended to collect around the bridge trestles along the slow-moving river. These items provided additional fuel for the flames, and the water itself was full of petroleum and other industrial runoff from steel plants.

Two months after the 1969 Cuyahoga River fire, *Time* magazine published a major article about it. By 1969, there was a growing ecology movement, and the general public was becoming concerned about lasting damage being done to the country's waterways. The *Time* article encapsulated these fears, complete with horrifying photographs, and Cleveland—specifically the Cuyahoga—became the symbol for industrial pollution.

The fire of 1969 was a turning point for the environmental movement. In 1972, Congress passed the Federal Water Pollution Control Amendments, also known as the Clean Water Act. This began to regulate the disposal of industrial waste and by-products, and it required cities to improve sewage treatment plants and processes and monitor the storm water and overflow.

Q. What deadly natural disaster occurred in Galveston, Texas, in September 1900?

A. Many remember Hurricane Sandy and Hurricane Katrina with horror, but the 1900 Galveston hurricane and flood was far more deadly.

Galveston is an island city that basks in the sun about an hour southeast of Houston. Every three years or so, Galveston can expect a brush with a major storm. Every ten years, it's likely to receive a direct hurricane hit.

Usually, the city breezes through those storms with ease. But September 8, 1900, was another story.

Unprepared and Vulnerable
In 1900, tropical storms and hurricanes weren't assigned names. Galveston residents knew that bad weather was coming, but the U.S. Weather Bureau discouraged use of terms such as *hurricane*. In addition, geographers claimed that the slope of the sea bottom protected the city against harsh ocean conditions. Galveston, the fourth-most-populous city in the state at the time, didn't even have a seawall.

By the time the Category 4 hurricane hit the city, fewer than half its residents had evacuated. In fact, the city was busy with tourists who'd arrived to enjoy the warm gulf waters and watch the eerie, oncoming clouds.

To date, Galveston's 1900 flood, which resulted from that storm, is America's worst natural disaster. It killed approximately 8,000 people with a 15-foot storm surge that destroyed roughly half of Galveston's homes and businesses and devastated the surrounding area. The flood has been the subject of books, movies, and songs. In 1904, crowds lined up to see the "Galveston Flood" attraction at New York's Coney Island. Most people don't realize, however, that the storm's damage extended far beyond Galveston.

A Wide Swath

During the 18-hour storm, the winds were so intense that telegraph lines as far away as Abilene—more than 300 miles from Galveston—were leveled. Between the Gulf of Mexico and Abilene, the 1900 storm snapped trees and crushed houses. On J. E. Dick's ranch near Galveston, 2,500 cattle drowned. Throughout East Texas, cities and towns were destroyed. Katy is just one of them.

Today, Katy is an upscale community about 25 miles west of Houston and 60 miles inland from Galveston. But the 1900 hurricane almost wiped Katy off the map. Only two houses were undamaged when the winds blew through the town's streets and swept homes and businesses from their foundations. Today, those two homes—Featherston House and Wright House—are part of Katy Heritage Park.

Houston was also in the storm's path. Much of the area's economy relied on farms and ranches that were ill prepared for the devastation that was coming. Winds and rising waters destroyed almost every barn in the hurricane's path. Waters up to 10 feet deep flooded local pastures. Across East Texas, entire forests were crushed. One news reporter observed, "no large timber left standing as far as the eye can see."

From there, it's not clear whether the storm headed due north or if it doubled back. Many believe it retraced its path to the Florida Keys and then continued up the East Coast. By the time it reached New York City, the winds were still raging at 65 miles per hour.

Digging Out
In the aftermath of the storm, the Galveston community dredged sand to raise the city up to 17 feet above sea level. The city also built a 17-foot-tall seawall to protect it from storm surges. Likewise, Houston and the cities around it improved drainage and created reservoirs and flood plains to absorb the water from future storms that were sure to come.

Q. Who was Typhoid Mary?

A. There were hundreds, if not thousands, of typhoid carriers in New York at the turn of the 20th century. Only one of them, however, was labeled a menace to society and banished to an island for life.

The popular image of Typhoid Mary in the early 1900s— an image enthusiastically promoted by the tabloids of the day—was of a woman stalking the streets of New York, infecting and killing hundreds of hapless victims. In truth, Mary Mallon, the woman who came to be recognized as Typhoid Mary, is known to have infected 47 people, 3 of whom died.

Mary Mallon immigrated to the United States from Ireland in 1883 at age 15. For a time, she lived with an aunt in New York City, but soon began working as a domestic servant, one of the few avenues of gainful employment open to a poor young woman of the day. Sometime before the turn of the century, she must have contracted and then recovered from a mild case of typhoid. Since a mild case of typhoid can mimic the symptoms of the flu, it is quite possible that she never even knew she had contracted the disease.

Mallon, an excellent cook, was working in the kitchens of the city's wealthiest families. In August 1906, she was hired by banker Charles Warren to cook for his family at their rented summer home on Long Island. After six of the eleven people in the house fell ill with typhoid, George Soper, a sanitary engineer, was hired by Charles Warren's landlord to pinpoint the source of the outbreak. Soper's attention eventually focused on the cook. After months of tracing Mary Mallon's job history, Soper discovered that typhoid had struck seven of the eight families for whom she'd cooked.

In March 1907, Mallon was working at a home on Park Avenue when George Soper paid a visit. Soper told Mary that she was a possible typhoid carrier and requested samples of her blood, urine, and feces for testing.

The idea that a healthy person could pass a disease on to others was barely understood by the general public at the time. For someone like Mary Mallon, who prided herself on never being sick, Soper's requests seemed particularly outrageous. Believing herself falsely accused, she picked up a carving fork and angrily forced Soper out of the house.

Because Mallon refused to submit voluntarily to testing, the New York Health Department called in the police. Officers dragged her into an ambulance and, with the city health inspector sitting on top of her, took her kicking and screaming to the Willard Parker Hospital. Tests revealed high concentrations of *typhoid bacilli* in her blood.

Quarantine

Declaring her a public menace, the health department moved Mallon to an isolation cottage on the grounds of the Riverside Hospital on North Brother Island in the East River. She had broken no laws and had not been given a trial, but she remained in quarantine for nearly three years.

In 1909, Mallon sued the health department for her freedom, insisting that she was healthy and that her banishment was illegal and unjustified. The judge ruled against Mallon, and she was sent back to Brother Island. In 1910, a new health department inspector freed her on the condition that she never work as a cook again. Mallon kept her promise for a time, but eventually returned to the only profession she knew that could offer her a decent income.

A 1915 typhoid outbreak at Sloane Maternity Hospital in New York City killed 2 people and infected 25 others. An investigation revealed that a recently hired cook named "Mary Brown" was in fact Mary Mallon. Mallon was immediately returned to her lonely cottage on Brother Island, where she remained quarantined until her death in 1938.

Historians have debated why Mallon was treated so differently than hundreds of other typhoid carriers. At the time of her first arrest, there were 3,000–4,500 new cases of typhoid each year in New York City. Approximately three percent of typhoid fever victims became carriers, which translated to roughly 100 new carriers per year. The city would have gone bankrupt had it tried to quarantine even a handful of them as it did Mallon.

Why Mary?

Typhoid Mary was not even the deadliest carrier. A man named Tony Labella was responsible for 122 cases and

5 deaths in the 1920s. Despite the fact that he handled food and was uncooperative with authorities, he was isolated for only two weeks and then released. A bakery and restaurant owner named Alphonse Cotils was also a carrier. In 1924, Cotils was arrested after officials discovered him inside his restaurant after being warned to stay away from food. Cotils was released after promising to conduct his business by phone.

So why was Mary Mallon forced into a life of quarantine when others were not? For one thing, Mallon was the first discovered healthy carrier of typhoid. At the time, Mallon, like most people, didn't understand that a healthy person could be a carrier of the disease, so she saw no reason to change her behavior. Mallon's use of an assumed name in the Sloane Maternity Hospital case was also seen by the public as a deliberate act, maliciously designed to put others at risk.

Some historians suspect that Mallon's fate was tied to the fact that she was a single female and an Irish immigrant. Prejudice against the Irish still ran high at the time, and it was considered unnatural—if not immoral—for a woman to remain single all her life. Another strike against Mary Mallon was her work as a domestic servant. Diseases like typhoid fever were associated with the unclean habits of the "lower classes." These factors combined to transform Mary Mallon from a simple woman into the menacing, legendary Typhoid Mary—a threat that had to be contained.

Q. **Which Hawaiian Island has the state's most unusual waterfall?**

A. Hawaii's third largest island, Oahu, touts the state's most unusual waterfall—one that defies gravity.

Tears in the Mist

The lush Nu'uanu Valley on the eastern coast of Oahu stretches from Honolulu to the Ko'olau Range and ends quite suddenly in steep cliffs, called the Pali.

Here, on only the rainiest and windiest of days, visitors can see the famous Upside-Down Waterfall, so called because water cascading from the 3,150-foot summit of Mount Konahuanui falls only a few feet before strong trade winds blow it back up in the air. The water dissipates into mist, creating the illusion of water slowly falling upward.

Natives call the waterfall *Waipuhia*, or "blown water." According to one legend, Waipuhia was named for a young local girl whose bright eyes pleased the gods. One tragic day, the girl's true love was lost in a storm, and when she wept for him, her tears were caught halfway down the cliff by the god of wind and tossed into the spray by the god of mist.

Lookout Lore

Weather permitting, the best view of the waterfall is from the 1,186-foot Nu'uanu Pali Lookout, itself an infamous spot in Hawaiian lore. As the legend goes, in 1795, King Kamehameha I drove the Oahu warriors up the Nu'uanu Valley to the Pali, where thousands of them were driven over the cliffs to their deaths.

While scholars pooh-pooh the story, natives say that at night the cries of long-dead warriors can be heard echoing through the valley. Others tell of seeing ghost warriors falling from cliffs as well as a ghostly white figure—perhaps the king—on the paved road that today leads up to the Lookout. Now called the Pali Highway, that road was built in 1898. Apparently, Wilson's workers encountered several bones during the project—and simply laid the road right over them.

Q. What American microbiologist developed disease-resistant wheat varieties that saved billions of people from starvation?

A. Norman Ernest Borlaug (1914–2009). This American microbiologist and agricultural scientist was instrumental in developing high-yield, disease-resistant wheat varieties in Latin America, Africa, and Asia. Borlaug effectively saved billions of people from starvation and was awarded the Nobel Peace Prize in 1970. According to the Congressional Tribute to Dr. Norman E. Borlaug Act of 2006, "Dr. Borlaug has saved more lives than any other person who has ever lived."

Q. Where did America send its lepers?

A. Life has never been easy for lepers. Throughout history, they've been stigmatized, feared, and cast out by society. Such reactions—though undeniably heartless—were perhaps understandable because the disease was thought to be rampantly contagious. Anyone suspected of leprosy was forced into quarantine and left to die.

Leprosy has affected humanity since at least 600 B.C. This miserable disease, now known as Hansen's disease, attacks the nervous system primarily in the hands, feet, and face and causes disfiguring skin sores, nerve damage, and progressive debilitation. Medical science had no understanding of leprosy until the late 1800s and no effective treatment for it until the 1940s. Prior to that point, lepers faced a slow, painful, and certain demise.

Misinterpretations of biblical references to leprosy in Leviticus 13:45–46, which labeled lepers as "unclean" and dictated that sufferers must "dwell apart . . . outside the camp," didn't help matters. (The "leprosy" cited in Leviticus referred to several skin conditions, but Hansen's disease was not one of them.) It's really no surprise that society's less-than-compassionate response to the disease was the leper colony.

Cast Out in Misery and Despair
The first leper colonies were isolated spots in the wilderness where the afflicted were driven, forgotten, and left to die.

The practice of exiling lepers continued well into the 20th century. In Crete, for instance, lepers were banished to mountainside caves, where they survived by eating scraps left by wolves. More humane measures were adopted in 1903 when lepers were corralled into the Spinalonga Island leper colony and given food and shelter and cared for by priests and nuns. However, once you entered, you never left, and it remained that way until the colony's last resident died in 1957.

Still, joining a leper colony sometimes beat living among the healthy. It wasn't much fun wandering from town to town while wearing signs or ringing bells to warn of one's affliction. And you were always susceptible to violence from townsfolk gripped by irrational fear—as when lepers were blamed for epidemic outbreaks and thrown into bonfires as punishment.

Life in the American Colony
American attitudes toward lepers weren't any more enlightened. One of modern time's most notorious leper colonies was on the Hawaiian island of Molokai, which was established in 1866.

Hawaiian kings and American officials banished sufferers to this remote peninsula ringed by jagged lava rock and towering sea cliffs. Molokai became one of the world's largest leper colonies—its population peaked in 1890 at 1,174—and more than 8,000 people were forcibly confined there before the practice was finally ended in 1969.

The early days of Molokai were horrible. The banished were abandoned in a lawless place where they received minimal care and had to fight with others for food, water, blankets, and shelter. Public condemnation led to improved conditions on Molokai, but residents later became freaks on display as Hollywood celebrities flocked to the colony on macabre sightseeing tours.

A Leper Haven in Louisiana

While sufferers of leprosy were being humiliated in Hawaii, they were being helped in Louisiana.

In 1894, the Louisiana Leper House, which billed itself as "a place of treatment and research, not detention," opened in Carville. In 1920, it was transferred to federal authority and renamed the National Leprosarium of the United States. Known today as the National Hansen's Disease Program (NHDP), the facility became a leading research and rehabilitation center, pioneering treatments that form the basis of multidrug therapies currently prescribed by the World Health Organization (WHO) for the treatment of Hansen's disease.

It was here that researchers enlisted a common Louisiana critter—the armadillo—in the fight against the disease. It had always been difficult to study Hansen's disease. Human nerves are seldom biopsied, so direct data on nerve damage from Hansen's was minimal. But in the 1960s, NHDP researchers theorized that armadillos might be susceptible to the germ because of their low body temperature. They began inoculating armadillos with it and discovered that the animals could develop the disease systemically. Now the armadillo is used to develop infected nerves for research worldwide.

A Thing of the Past?
In 1985, leprosy was still considered a public health problem in 122 countries. In fact, the last remaining leper colony, located in Croatia, didn't close until 2002. However, WHO has made great strides toward eradicating the disease and indicated in 2000 that the rate of infection had dropped by 90 percent. The multidrug therapies currently prescribed for the treatment of leprosy are available to all patients for free via WHO. Approximately four million patients have been cured since 2000.

Q. What were some of New York City's worst catastrophes?

A. **Yellow Fever Epidemics:** The city was struck by the mosquito-borne virus in 1668, 1702, 1794–95, 1798, 1803, 1819, and 1822. Some of the outbreaks killed hundreds; others killed thousands. The outbreak of 1798, with more than 2,000 deaths, was the worst.

Great Fire of New York: This conflagration that consumed the west side of southern Manhattan started on September 21, 1776, probably in a waterfront tavern, during the colonial defense of the city against the British. Some 400 to 500 buildings were destroyed.

Chatham Street Fire: On May 19, 1811, high winds gusting to gale force turned a factory blaze into a pyre for 100 buildings. A general shortage of water available to firefighters was an early wake-up call about the city's future needs.

Long Island Hurricane: The first major hurricane in the city's history hit at Jamaica Bay on September 3, 1821. The 13-foot storm surge flooded Battery Park and lower Manhattan as far as Canal Street. While damaging, the flood caused few deaths.

Cholera Epidemics: In 1832, 1848–49, and 1866, cholera outbreaks killed thousands at a time. Indelicately put, the ailment killed with diarrhea that led to irreversible fluid loss. Early treatments included opium suppositories and tobacco enemas—neither of which is recommended for home treatment today!

Great Financial District Fire: On December 16–17, 1835, city firefighters discovered that water is very hard to pump when the air temperature is 17 degrees Fahrenheit. This largely unchecked blaze incinerated 500 buildings around Wall Street, including most of the few remaining Dutch-era structures.

***Westfield II* Ferry Explosion:** The boiler of this Staten Island steamer blew up at Manhattan dockside on July 30, 1871, killing 125 and injuring about 140.

Brooklyn Theatre Fire: On December 5, 1876, theatergoers who had gathered to see a popular French melodrama, *The Two Orphans*, were sent into panic when fire broke out at the Brooklyn Theatre. Many of the 278 dead were children in the cheap seats, where fire-escape provisions were inadequate.

Great Blizzard of 1888: New York tried to absorb snowdrifts of 20 feet or more and winds in excess of 45 miles per hour, when a late-winter storm slammed the

Atlantic coast from Maryland to Maine. Two hundred of the storm's 400 deaths occurred in New York City.

Heat Wave of 1896: During the long span of August 5–13, sustained temperatures above 90 degrees Fahrenheit scorched people in tenements, sometimes lethally. In the end, 420 or more people died, mostly in the overcrowded squalor of the Lower East Side.

***General Slocum* Disaster:** Until 9/11, June 15, 1904, was New York's deadliest day. During a church picnic aboard a chartered steamboat in the East River, more than 1,000 people, most of them German-American women and children, died when the triple-deck, wooden ship caught fire.

Triangle Shirtwaist Fire: On March 25, 1911, a carelessly tossed match or cigarette started a fast-spreading fire inside Max Blanck and Isaac Harris's shirtwaist (blouse) sweatshop, which occupied the eighth, ninth, and tenth floors of Manhattan's Asch Building. Grossly inadequate fire exit provisions, plus locked inner doors, spelled disaster. Most of the 146 dead were immigrant women, mainly Jewish. Those that did not burn to death died of smoke inhalation or from injuries sustained when they leapt from windows.

Wall Street Bombing: Was it a car bomb that exploded in the financial district on September 16, 1920? No, it was a horse-drawn wagon bomb carrying 100 pounds of dynamite and hundreds of pounds of iron that went up in front of 23 Wall Street. The massive explosion killed 38 people and wounded more than 300. No perpetrator was ever found, but authorities unofficially blamed two popular bogeymen of the day—anarchists and Communists.

Holland Tunnel Fire: New York City officials have good reasons for banning highly explosive carbon disulfide from being driven through the Holland Tunnel. On Friday, May 13, 1949, a 55-gallon drum of the solvent fell off a truck and caught fire. The blaze spread quickly, engulfing many of the 125 vehicles that were in the tunnel at the time, and ravaging the structure's ceiling and walls. An FDNY battalion chief was felled by smoke and died four months later. Sixty-six people were injured.

TWA Flight 266/United Flight 826: Snow, rain, and fog, plus pilot error, precipitated the December 16, 1960, midair collision of a TWA Constellation and a United DC-8 some 5,200 feet above the city. United Flight 826 had been badly off course. The DC-8 fell onto Brooklyn's Park Slope neighborhood, killing six people on the ground. The Constellation disintegrated on impact and crashed at Miller Field on Staten Island. All 128 people on the two planes perished, although an 11-year-old boy aboard the DC-8 survived long enough to describe the crash to authorities.

Eastern Airlines Flight 66: On June 24, 1975, a Boeing 727 attempting to land at JFK International Airport was knocked to the earth short of the runway by freak wind shear caused by a thunderstorm. Seven passengers and two flight attendants survived; the other 115 passengers and crew did not.

1977 Blackout: Except for south Queens, all of NYC lost power on July 13–14, 1977, when a lightning strike sent electrical grids into a tizzy. Unlike the famed 1965 blackout, which was notable for its peaceful nature, this one encouraged widespread looting, arson, and vandalism. More than 3,700 people were arrested, and hundreds of police were injured.

World Trade Center Garage Bombing: On February 26, 1993, Islamic terrorists detonated 1,500 pounds of explosives in a lower-level garage, killing six people. Over 1,000 were injured, mostly during the towers' frantic evacuation.

TWA Flight 800: A Boeing 747 out of JFK Airport with 230 people aboard blew up south of Long Island on July 17, 1996. There were no survivors, but numerous conspiracy theories made the rounds. The FBI found no evidence of a criminal act, and the National Transportation Safety Board attributed the crash to an electrical spark that ignited fuel vapors in a wing tank.

World Trade Center Attacks: September 11, 2001, will live in infamy as the nation's worst terrorist attack. Two airliners hijacked by Islamic extremists were flown into Manhattan, where each of the planes struck one of the twin towers of the World Trade Center, which ultimately collapsed. A total of 2,751 died, and over 6,000 were injured—many of the casualties were police and firefighters. (On the same morning, another hijacked airliner crashed into the Pentagon, and a fourth crashed in rural Pennsylvania.)

American Flight 587: Freak physics and some operator over-reaction were the causes of the November 12, 2001, crash of an Airbus A300 just minutes out of JFK International Airport. The American Airlines flight took off in a wake of intense turbulence left by a larger 747. The pilots' struggle with the rudder led to catastrophic structural failure. The vertical stabilizer sheared off, followed by both engines. What remained of the plane went down in the Belle Harbor neighborhood of Queens, demolishing houses and killing five people. In all, 265 people lost their lives.

Q. What woman helped defeat the yellow fever epidemic during the Spanish-American War?

A. Clara Maass. Today the name Clara Maass is not well known. But at the turn of the century, practically everyone in the United States knew her as the nurse who risked her own life to help defeat the dreaded yellow fever epidemic.

Young Girl Grows Up

Clara Louise Maass was born in East Orange, New Jersey, on June 28, 1876. She was the daughter of German immigrants who quickly discovered upon their arrival in America that the streets were not paved with gold. The family was just barely getting by.

Clara began working while she was still in grammar school. At around age 16, she enrolled in nursing school at Newark German Hospital in Newark, New Jersey. Graduating from the rigorous course in 1895, she continued working hard. By 1898, she was the head nurse at Newark German.

Yellow Jack War

The Spanish-American War began on February 15, 1898. As wars go, the war was more period than paragraph, lasting just four short months. However, there was something more deadly to American troops than Spanish bullets—yellow fever.

Since its arrival in America in the summer of 1693, yellow fever had ravaged the country. For two centuries, "Yellow

Jack," as the disease was dubbed, killed randomly and indiscriminately. The disease would devastate some households, while those next door would go untouched. One in ten people were killed by yellow fever in Philadelphia in 1793. The disease caused President George Washington and the federal government (Philadelphia was then the U.S. capitol) to flee the city. In 1802, Yellow Jack killed 23,000 French troops in Haiti, causing Napoleon to abandon the New World (and eventually agree to the Louisiana Purchase). An 1878 outbreak in Memphis killed 5,000 people there, and 20,000 total died in the Mississippi Delta. No one knew what caused yellow fever or how to stop it.

The Experiments
In April 1898, Maass applied to become a contract nurse during the Spanish-American War. In Santiago, Cuba, she saw her first cases of yellow fever. The next year she battled the disease in Manila, as it ravaged the American troops there.

No one knew why Maass kept going to these danger zones when she could have remained safely at home nurturing her burgeoning nursing career. Yet when Havana was hit by a severe yellow fever epidemic in 1900, Maass once again answered a call for nurses to tend the sick.

In Havana, a team of doctors led by Walter Reed was trying to find the cause of yellow fever. They had reason to support a controversial theory that mosquitoes were the disease carrier, but they needed concrete proof. Desperate, they asked for human volunteers, offering to pay them $100—and another $100 if they became ill. Maass volunteered for the tests, though no one is sure why she put herself up to it. She may have hoped that contracting a mild case of the disease would give her immunity to it and allow her to better treat patients.

On August 14, 1901, after a previous mosquito bite had produced just a mild case of sickness, a willing Maass was bitten once again by an *Aedes aegypti* mosquito loaded with infectious blood. This time the vicious disease tore through her body. She wrote a feverish last letter home to her family: "You know I am the man of the family but pray for me . . ."

On August 24, Maass died. Her death ended the controversial practice of using humans as test subjects for experiments. But it also proved, beyond a doubt, that the *Aedes aegypti* mosquito was the disease carrier—the key to unlocking the sickness that scientists had been seeking for centuries. Yellow fever could finally be conquered, in part because of Maass's brave sacrifice.

The next day, a writer for the *New York Journal* wrote, "No soldier in the late war placed his life in peril for better reasons than those which prompted this faithful nurse to risk hers."

Q. ■ Was the Three Mile Island nuclear accident as bad as the Chernobyl incident?

A. ■ No. The nuclear accident at Three Mile Island in Pennsylvania the late 1970s gripped the country and caused panic throughout the region, but it was no Chernobyl.

The incident at Three Mile Island was caused by a failure involving the water pumps. This in turn caused pressure to build up inside the core of the reactor. This pressure caused a relief valve to open. The relief valve failed to close again, however, and cooling water was released from the reactor. This caused the core of the reactor to overheat. Because the operators did not realize that the plant was experiencing a loss-of-coolant accident, they made conditions worse by further reducing the flow of coolant through the core. Consequently, the nuclear fuel overheated to the point where the long metal tubes that hold the nuclear fuel pellets ruptured and the fuel pellets began to melt. Though the Nuclear Regulatory Commission (NRC) calls the accident "the most serious in the U.S. commercial nuclear power plant operating history," no lives were lost and the amount of radiation released was within safe levels.

As bad as the Three Mile Island event was, it pales in comparison to the accident at the Chernobyl nuclear power plant just outside the town of Pripyat, Ukraine, on April 26, 1986. At Chernobyl, workers were performing a test to see how the reactor would fare in the case of an electrical failure, and a design flaw in the reactor caused a power surge. The surge set off two explosions. As the reactor was not surrounded by any kind of containment structure, the explosions sent a significant amount of radioactive material into the atmosphere. Chernobyl remains the largest nuclear power plant disaster in history. The event directly killed 31 people; produced a massive plume of radioactive debris that drifted over parts of the western Soviet Union, Eastern Europe, and Scandinavia; left huge areas dangerously contaminated; and forced the evacuation of more than 200,000 people.

Q. Where is the Barringer Crater and how was it created?

A. Arizona. A 160-foot meteorite landed in the northern desert about 50,000 years ago, leaving an impact crater about a mile wide and 570 feet deep. Scientists believe the meteorite that caused the crater was traveling about 28,600 miles per hour when it struck Earth, causing an explosion about 150 times more powerful than the Hiroshima atomic bomb. The meteorite itself probably melted in the explosion, spreading a mist of molten nickel and iron across the surrounding landscape. The Barringer Crater, or Meteor Crater, is a popular tourist attraction.

Q. What natural disaster ravaged the Great Plains between 1931 and 1939?

A. The Dust Bowl. In 1931, a severe drought hit the Midwest and Great Plains, and dust from the overgrazed, over-farmed land began to blow—causing intense dust storms. With no crops or prairie grasses to hold down depleted topsoil, high winds endemic to the area whipped dried dirt and soil into the air—in 1935 alone, officials estimated that some 850 million tons of topsoil had been blown off the land. The ecological disaster lasted for years at the height of the Great Depression. Affecting 100 million acres of the Great Plains, it brought poverty and malnutrition to millions and spurred an exodus of poor farmers to the West Coast. For years, the plains region had enjoyed high grain prices and phenomenal crops, but farmers had been overproducing for more than a generation. Overgrazing by cattle and sheep had further stripped the landscape. By 1930, 33 million acres of southern plains once held in place by native prairie grasses had been laid bare. The crisis began in 1931. Farmers enjoyed another bumper crop of wheat, but the resulting surplus forced prices down. Many farmers went broke, and others abandoned their fields just at the start of a severe drought that would last much of the decade. It wasn't until 1939 that rain returned and life improved.

Q. What is April 14, 1935, called in history books?

A. Black Sunday. Sunday April 14, 1935, began as a clear, pleasant day over much of the Midwest. But within hours, daytime would be transformed to night as a weather front with 60-mile-per-hour winds threw up a monstrous dust cloud from the barren fields of the Dust Bowl, burying homes in millions of tons of dirt.

People in the small towns and farms of Kansas, Oklahoma, Texas, and Colorado were used to dust storms and were ready to seal windows, doors, and every possible crack in their houses with sheets, blankets, and newspapers. But this particular storm, which came to be known as Black Sunday, was different. In Dodge City, Kansas, a strange nighttime fell for 40 minutes in the middle of the day, followed by three hours of near darkness. Inside their homes, men, women, and children huddled with handkerchiefs or wet sponges over their noses, struggling to breathe. Many believed the world was ending. A few hours later in Chicago, the cloud dumped three pounds of soil for each person in the city. The next day, it blanketed New York and Washington, D.C., before sweeping out into the Atlantic Ocean. The Black Sunday storm was the worst of the Dust Bowl.

Stormy Weather

In 1932, 14 dust storms—whipped skyward by strong, dry winds—were reported in the United States. The following year, the storms numbered 38, and a region centering on Oklahoma, Kansas, and northern Texas was dubbed the Dust Bowl. The first great storm occurred in May 1934, when high winds swirled 300,000 tons of soil from Montana and Wyoming skyward. By evening, the "black blizzard" began depositing dust like snow on the streets of Chicago. By dawn the next day, the cloud had rolled eastward over New York, Washington, D.C., and Atlanta, dimming the sun before moving out to sea and dusting ships 300 miles off shore. In the Midwest, summer temperature records were broken as thousands of livestock starved and suffocated. Hundreds of people died from heat stroke, malnutrition, and dust pneumonia.

Black Sunday

In March 1935, another big storm blew topsoil from the fields of Kansas, Colorado, Texas, and Oklahoma all the way to the East Coast, but it was only a prelude of what was to come.

Twenty huge dust storms tore through the region on April 14, 1935, converging in a single front headed east. Witnesses reported that at times they could not see five feet in front of them. A pilot who encountered a dust cloud at 20,000 feet assumed it was a thunderstorm. She tried to climb above it, but could not, and had to turn back. In Oklahoma and Texas, humble homesteads were literally buried beneath feet of dust.

When the dust settled, a drastic migration began that would culminate in 15 percent of Oklahomans leaving the state. Called "Okies" in California, the uprooted people searching for a new life actually came from all the states of the Midwest affected by the continuing disaster.

Working for the Farm Security Administration, photographer Dorothea Lange documented their lives, while novelist John Steinbeck immortalized their plight with *The Grapes of Wrath*.

Aftermath

Black Sunday would be an impetus for change. With dirt from the storm still falling over Washington, D.C., Hugh Hammond Bennett—a soil surveyor from North Carolina who helped found the soil conservation movement—won the support of Congress, which declared soil erosion a national menace. Later that year, President Roosevelt signed into law the Soil Conservation Act of 1935, establishing Soil Conservation Service in the Department of Agriculture. Under Bennett's direction, an aggressive campaign to stabilize the region's soil began. Roosevelt also undertook banking reforms and other agricultural policies to help rescue the plains farmers. One of his decisions led to the planting of more than 222,000 trees.

For the next year, however, the drought continued, as summer temperatures soared to 120 degrees. Sporadic rains and floods in 1937 and 1938 joined the continuing dust storms, and wintertime brought a new kind of storm called a "snuster"—a mixture of dirt and snow reaching blizzard proportions. The fall of 1939 finally brought the rains that ended the drought. With new farming methods and increased agricultural demand due to World War II, the Great Plains once again became golden with wheat.

Q. **What is the famous archaeological and fossil site in the heart of Los Angeles?**

A. The La Brea Tar Pits. As the ocean that once covered California began to recede about

100,000 years ago, older fossil fuels began to seep toward the earth's surface. In La Brea, this took the form of "asphalt," an extremely sticky, tarlike substance. It formed swamplike  conditions roughly 40,000 years ago that trapped animals wandering through the area. Predators spotting them would give chase and get stuck in the asphalt themselves. The unique chemical nature of asphalt protected these animals' bones from deterioration, which gives modern-day scientists pristine examples of prehistoric mammal skeletons, such as mammoths and mastodons, American camels and American lions, and saber-toothed cats.

Q. Why does sourdough bread taste better in San Francisco?

A. The secret is in the air. A strain of wild microorganisms called *Lactobacillus sanfrancisco* that flourish in San Francisco's mild, damp climate lends a unique tangy flavor to the bread during the leavening process. Sourdough bakers in other locales can't achieve the same tangy flavor without *Lactobacillus sanfrancisco*.

To make sourdough bread, San Francisco bakers start by mixing flour and water in a bowl. The mixture attracts yeasts, *Lactobacillus sanfrancisco*, and other bacteria from the air. The microorganisms feed on the flour and begin to multiply. At the same time, the yeasts emit carbon dioxide, which causes the dough to rise, and the bacteria produce vinegar and lactic acid. The vinegar and lactic acid also contribute to the unique flavor of San Francisco sourdough.

Sourdough bread has been around since 1500 B.C., when the Egyptians first discovered leavening agents. It became a true taste treat when it arrived in San Francisco in the mid-19th century, about the time of the California Gold Rush. San Francisco's first sourdough bakers, the Boudin family, opened shop in 1849, and soon dozens of other bakeries cropped up, including Parisian, Toscana, and Colombo.

If you don't live in San Francisco, don't fret. You can still enjoy the taste of San Francisco sourdough bread at home. Pure cultures of *Lactobacillus sanfrancisco* are freeze-dried and supplied to bakeries around the world.

Q. What happened to the Mercury 13 mission?

A. The first U.S. astronauts were the renowned Mercury Seven. But they were followed fairly quickly by the Mercury 13. Never heard of them?

In 1961, a group of highly qualified women were selected for astronaut flight training. They passed every test and endured every poke, prod, and simulation. In some cases, they actually fared better than their male counterparts. But was America really ready to send women into space? Apparently not.

The Soviets fired the starter's gun in the space race by launching the *Sputnik* satellite on October 4, 1957. Threatened by the Soviets' ability to beat them to the punch, the United States accelerated their own space initiatives, including the formation of the National Aeronautics and Space Administration (NASA). Next time, the United States would be first.

There was much yet to learn about space. What could humans tolerate? Jet pilots required pressure suits; what of weightless space? What of the confinement? Military test pilots—fit, brave, and calm during flight crises—seemed logical candidates. Of course, since women weren't allowed to be military test pilots, they weren't considered for astronaut training. At least, not at first.

Secret Experiments
Freethinking researcher Dr. Randy Lovelace II helped screen the first seven male astronauts as part of the Mercury Seven program. Then Lovelace had a flash of inspiration, thinking: *A space rocket needs every joule of energy. Every gram of weight counts. Women are lighter; they use less oxygen and food. We know for sure they can fly; heck, Jackie Cochran helped me start my research foundation. Maybe they're actually better suited! Let's explore this!*

Cochran herself was well over the age limit of 35, but Oklahoman Geraldyn "Jerrie" Cobb wasn't. A record-setting aviator, Cobb had earned her private pilot's license when she was just 17 years old. Between 1957 and 1960, she set four aviation world records for speed, distance, and absolute altitude.

When Jerrie received an invitation from Dr. Lovelace to train for space flight, she dropped everything for what seemed like the opportunity of a lifetime. She arrived in Albuquerque in 1960 and began the torture tests. She underwent barium enemas and had all her body fluids sampled. Supercooled water was squirted into her ear canal to test her reaction to vertigo. She endured the infamous "Vomit Comet" spin simulator—and many more tests besides.

Cobb blew the trials away. When Lovelace announced this to the media, they fawned over the "astronette." Cobb was the first of 25 women tested for astronaut potential. Only some of the women met one another in person, but Cobb was involved in their recruitment and knew them all. Thirteen passed all the tests to become FLATs: Fellow Lady Astronaut Trainees, an acronym taken from Cobb's written salutation to them.

The women's next planned step was testing at navy facilities in Pensacola. Each went home to wait. But when Lovelace asked to use Pensacola, the navy called NASA. The organization was less than enthused about the female astronauts, so the navy pushed the training overboard.

In September 1961, each FLAT got a telegram: *Sorry, program cancelled. You may now resume your normal lives.*

The women couldn't have been more dismayed. All that work—for nothing! They didn't give up, but they also didn't coordinate their lobbying. Cobb, the FLATs' self-appointed spokesperson, didn't get along well with Cochran—who in turn had her own ideas. Cobb's appeals up the national chain of command were honest, impassioned, and naive. Cochran, with personal contacts ranging from Chuck Yeager to VP Lyndon Johnson, preferred to work gradually within the sexist system rather than have an open challenge slapped down. One FLAT, Jane Hart, was the wife of a U.S. senator and was arguably the savviest political spokesperson available. Hart fumed as Cochran testified to Congress that she was against a "special program for women."

Was It Ever Possible?

We can guess the outcome based on LBJ's reaction to the memo across his desk concerning the female astronauts. He scrawled: "LET'S STOP THIS NOW!" If President Kennedy's space tsar had that attitude, there had never been any real hope. The men leading the nation weren't ready to send women into space. Period.

Was Lovelace deluded? Give him credit for trying, but he also didn't clue NASA in until news of the Pensacola plans blindsided them, resulting in a reflex "no way." On the other hand, had he sought advance permission, odds of NASA giving it were unlikely.

On June 16, 1963, about a year after Cobb, Hart, and Cochran spoke before Congress, cosmonaut Valentina Tereshkova of the Soviet Union flew in space. She was not a test pilot but a parachute hobbyist. It would be 20 more years before the first American woman, Sally Ride, made it into space.

Founding the Nation

Q. On March 5, 1770, an angry mob began to collect at the Custom House in Boston, Massachusetts. What happened next?

A. The Boston Massacre. The confrontation started with curses and taunts against the soldiers and escalated into a barrage of snowballs and junk. Soon the mob was egging on the troops to fire. When Redcoat reinforcements arrived, their captain tried to calm the situation down, but someone (probably an angry Loyalist) behind the British line encouraged the soldiers to open fire. Just then, something—many accounts say it was a stick or hunk of wood—knocked a soldier down. He stood up and fired, and a ragged volley followed before the captain could stop it. The toll was three colonials dead, with two more dying from their injuries the next day, and half a dozen or so wounded.

Q. Most historians mark April 19, 1775, as the start of the American Revolution, when the "shot heard 'round the world" was fired. Where was that shot fired?

A. Lexington, Massachusetts. British troops, 700 strong, were advancing on Concord to destroy arms and munitions belonging to the patriots. At Lexington, they found 77 members of the local militia known as "Minutemen." Someone—to this day no one knows who—fired an unordered shot. The gunfire that followed resulted in eight Americans killed and eight wounded.

Q. Was Aaron Burr a hero or a villain?

A. Mention the name Aaron Burr and the thing most people remember is his famous duel with Alexander Hamilton. That may have been the high point of his life, because by the time Burr passed away in 1836, he was considered one of the most mistrusted public figures of his era.

How to Make Friends . . .

Burr seemed to have a knack for making enemies out of important people. George Washington disliked him so much from their time together during the Revolutionary War that as president, he had Burr banned from the National Archives, didn't appoint him as minister to France, and refused to make him a brigadier general.

After the war, Burr became a lawyer in New York, frequently opposing his future dueling partner Alexander Hamilton. But it wasn't until Burr beat Hamilton's father-in-law in the race for a Senate seat that the problems between them really started.

In 1800, Burr ran for president against Thomas Jefferson. Back then, the candidate with the most votes got to be president; whoever came in second became vice president—even if they were from different parties. When the election ended in a tie in the Electoral College, it was thrown to the House of Representatives to decide. After 35 straight tie votes, Jefferson was elected president, and Burr became vice president.

Like Washington, Jefferson didn't hold Burr in high regard. So in 1804, Burr decided to run for governor of New York. When he lost, he blamed the slandering of the press in general and the almost constant criticism from Hamilton in particular.

Hamilton later shot off at the mouth at a dinner party, and Burr decided he'd had enough. After giving Hamilton a chance to take his comments back (Hamilton refused), Burr challenged him to the famous duel.

I Challenge You to a Duel

On July 11, 1804, Burr and Hamilton met at Weehawken, New Jersey. Some say that Hamilton fired first, discharging his pistol into the air. Others say that he just missed. Burr, on the other hand, didn't miss, shooting Hamilton. He died the next day.

After the duel, Burr fled to his daughter's home in South Carolina until things cooled down. He was indicted for murder in both New York and New Jersey, but nothing ever came of it, and he eventually returned to Washington to finish his term as vice president. But his political career was over.

King Burr?

After his term as vice president, Burr decided to head west, to what was then considered Ohio and the new lands of the Louisiana Purchase. It seemed that Burr had things on his mind other than the scenery, however. According to some (mostly his rivals), Burr intended to create a new empire with himself as king. As the story goes, he planned to conquer a portion of Texas still held by Mexico, and then convince some of the existing western states to join his new confederacy. Called the Burr Conspiracy, it got the attention of President Jefferson, who issued arrest orders for treason. Eventually, Burr was captured and in 1807 was brought to trial.

But Burr caught a break. The judge was Chief Justice John Marshall. Marshall and Jefferson didn't get along, and rather than give his enemy an easy victory, Marshall demanded that the prosecution produce two witnesses that specifically heard Burr commit treason. The prosecution failed to come up with anybody, and Burr was set free.

Burr then left the United States to live in Europe. Returning to New York in 1812, he quietly practiced law until his death in 1836.

Q. Who said, "Give me liberty or give me death"?

A. Patrick Henry. The outspoken statesman was a self-taught lawyer and the first governor of the Commonwealth of Virginia. But poor health forced Henry to turn down several key governmental positions, including secretary of state under George Washington, chief justice of the Supreme Court, U.S. senator, and U.S. minister to France. He was elected to the Virginia legislature in 1799 but died before taking office.

Q. Why is Benedict Arnold's name synonymous with treason in the U.S.?

A. While serving as a general in the Continental Army during the Revolutionary War, Benedict Arnold switched sides when he offered to surrender the American fort at West Point, New York, to the British for £20,000 in 1780. Arnold had been a friend of George Washington and a hero of the Revolutionary War, but too many setbacks had made him frustrated. Arnold was in heavy debt and felt slighted in favor of mediocre officers. When he was passed over for a promotion and received a court-martial for violating military regulations, he went over to the side of the British, committing treason against the colonies and leading raids on former allies and friends.

Although Arnold's plot to surrender the American fort at West Point was stopped, the Americans did not capture him, and he became a brigadier general in the British Army. His unsavory reputation had followed him from Canada to England, making him a tolerated but unpopular figure. His postwar businesses hadn't thrived, and with Napoleon running amok, Arnold's death and burial in England were relatively insignificant.

On his deathbed in 1801, Benedict Arnold purportedly donned his old Continental Army togs and repented his treason with the words "Let me die in this old uniform in which I fought my battles. May God forgive me for ever having put on another."

Q. **Did Betsy Ross really stitch the first American flag?**

A. Schoolchildren are taught numerous things about the American Revolution that aren't necessarily supported by history. Among the debated stories is the "fact" that Betsy Ross stitched the first American flag.

Elizabeth (Betsy) Griscom was born in 1752 to a Quaker family, the eighth of 17 children. When she turned 21 in 1773, she eloped with an Episcopalian named John Ross, and because of their union, she was expelled from her congregation. Before they met, John and Betsy had both worked as apprentice upholsterers, so they decided to start their own business. Sadly, John died in January 1776 while serving with the Pennsylvania militia. The patriotic seamstress continued to run the business, and she soon expanded her efforts, making and mending gear for the Continental Army (a receipt exists that shows she made flags for the Pennsylvania State Navy in 1777).

So she could have sewn the first flag, but there's no proof that she actually did. In 1870, at a meeting of the Historical Society of Pennsylvania, Betsy's grandson, William Canby, insisted that George Washington had sought out Betsy and asked her to design and create a flag for the new country. Other Canby relatives swore out affidavits in agreement.

Suppose Washington had indeed asked her to make the first flag. When he became the first president, why didn't he do something to honor her? Why did her contribution never come up during her lifetime? Betsy Ross died in 1836, yet her family waited 34 years to announce her accomplishment. It could be that the family legend embellishes a grain of truth. Betsy Ross did make flags for the war effort, so she could have lived her life believing she had made the first American flag.

Q. The capital of the United States moved to Washington, D.C., in 1800. Where was it immediately before that?

A. Philadelphia. A rivalry between Northern and Southern advocates, who each pushed to have the capital in one of their regional states, had delayed the decision of a permanent location. In 1790, a compromise finally resolved the dispute, deciding that the capital would not be a part of any state. A site on the Potomac River was chosen and declared the District of Columbia. New York had been the nation's first capital, but as part of the compromise, the title moved to Philadelphia until the new capital was ready. Construction of the White House began in Washington in 1792, with work on the Capitol starting the following year.

Q. Who is known for the phrase, "I have not yet begun to fight"?

A. John Paul Jones, America's first naval hero. Entangled in a fierce battle with the British frigate *Serapis* in 1779, Jones's ship, the *Bonhomme Richard*, had taken severe damage. When the *Serapis*'s captain asked if he was ready to surrender, Jones yelled his immortal response: "I have not yet begun to fight!"

Q. Which Founding Father was called the "Master Builder of the Constitution"?

A. The 5'4" James Madison may have been short of stature, but he is a giant in American history. He drafted the "Virginia Plan," which became the basis of the Constitution. He took the floor more than 150 times at the Continental Congress to push tirelessly for a strong central government. (With Alexander Hamilton and John Jay, he also wrote The Federalist Papers, commenting on constitutional issues.)

Q. **Which Founding Father believed the Constitution should be rewritten every generation?**

A. Thomas Jefferson. In 1816, Jefferson wrote a letter to historian Samuel Kercheval, stating his belief that each generation has "a right to choose for itself the form of government it believes most promotive of its own happiness . . . and it is for the peace and good of mankind, that a solemn opportunity of doing this every nineteen or twenty years, should be provided by the constitution."

Q. **Did George Washington really tell his father, "I cannot tell a lie"?**

A. The first U.S. president was renowned for his honor and virtue, but this line was nothing but a fabrication by a biographer who wanted to spice up Washington's image. Mason Locke Weems, a fiery pastor and bookseller, published *The Life and Memorable Actions of George Washington* in 1800, a year after Washington's death. It was an instant hit and was republished several times, with each edition boasting additions to a section titled "Curious Anecdotes Laudable to Himself and Exemplary to his Countrymen." The fabricated cherry tree story was included in the fifth edition (1806) and every edition thereafter.

Q. **Where was Francis Scott Key when he began writing "The Star-Spangled Banner"?**

A. On a British naval ship in Chesapeake Bay. On September 13, 1814, the British were attacking Baltimore to gain control of its port. Key and an American military officer were aboard a truce ship negotiating the release of a doctor captured by the British. Although that mission was a success, Key and his two companions were held on that ship until the barrage against Baltimore reached an end. At first light the next morning, Key saw that the American flag continued to fly above Fort McHenry, meaning that the British attack had failed. He began writing his poem to commemorate that fact before he left the British ship.

Although Key wrote the lyrics to the song (originally in the form of a poem), he did not compose the music. His lyrics were set to the tune of an old British song called "To Anacreon in Heaven."

Q. **Why did John Hancock sign his name so big on the Declaration of Independence?**

A. Poor John Hancock—he was the president of the Continental Congress as the United States sprang to life, and a nine-term governor of Massachusetts. Heck, he even graduated from Harvard. But what's his legacy? Penmanship.

Take a look at the Declaration of Independence—specifically, the 56 signatures affixed on the document that formally kicked off the American Revolution. You'll notice that one name stands out from the rest. It's written in large, flamboyant script in the center of the page directly below the main body of text.

That signature, of course, belongs to John Hancock, and it is the most readily recognized autograph on one of the most revered pieces of paper in American history. Hancock's inscription is so well known that his name has become synonymous with the word signature, as in "put your John Hancock on the dotted line."

One of the reasons Hancock's signature is so enormous is that he, as president of the Continental Congress, was the first to sign the Declaration of Independence. Hancock had plenty of real estate, and he used it. But goodness gracious, there were 55 other signatures that needed to be added. Leave some room, guy.

Still, it wasn't necessarily a case of a man doing something simply because he could. Hancock felt that a big signature was important. Signing such a document did two things. First, it told American colonists and the rest of the world why the Congress felt it was necessary to break away from Great Britain. Second, by creating the Declaration of Independence, the congressional members were directly insulting England's King George III, a treasonous act that could lead to hanging. Hancock believed that a bold sweep of his feathered quill would instill confidence and courage into his fellow colonial delegates, and into everyone else who read the document.

It's been said that after signing his name, Hancock defiantly exclaimed, "There, I guess King George will be able to read that!" or "The British ministry can read that name without spectacles; let them double the reward for my head!" Sure, and George Washington never told a lie. In all likelihood, Hancock never made such a boast—there simply wasn't the audience for it. Only one other person was present when Hancock signed the Declaration of Independence—Charles Thomson of Pennsylvania, the secretary of the Continental Congress, who claimed that Hancock never uttered such words. Besides, saying something that grandiose with just one other person in the room would have been, well, kind of weird.

The delegates voted for the Declaration of Independence on the night of July 4, 1776, but they did not sign it. (Now, go out and use that piece of info to win a bar bet!) The first version was printed, copied, signed by Hancock and Thomson, and distributed to political and military leaders for their review. On July 19, the Congress ordered that the document be "fairly engrossed on parchment," a fancy way of saying officially written. On August 2, the final version was ready to be signed. Hancock signed first, putting his John, er, his name in the middle of the document below the text. As was the custom, others started signing their names below Hancock's.

Not everyone whose name is on the Declaration of Independence was present that day. Signatures were added in the coming days, weeks, months, and years. The last person to sign was Thomas McKean, in 1781. And you just know that when McKean saw what little

room there was for his signature, he thought,
"[Bleeping] Hancock!"

Q. What Puritan town in New England is known for the unusual accusations and trials that were held there in 1692?

A. Salem, Massachusetts. Betty Parris and Abigail Williams started behaving strangely—throwing things, crawling under tables, crying, shaking, and complaining of being pricked by pins (behavior most modern parents would identify as a tantrum). They claimed they were being tormented by the specters of three outcast women from the town—the homeless Sarah Good, the immoral Sarah Osborne, and the Caribbean slave Tituba. All three were immediately arrested. Over the next year Betty Parris and Abigail Williams, along with several other town children, accused dozens more townspeople of witchcraft. The accused were tried in a specially commissioned court by witchcraft "experts" and almost universally sentenced to death by hanging. By the time the governor of the colony put an end to the madness, 25 or more innocent people had died—19 by hanging.

Q. Who said, "I only regret that I have but one life to lose for my country"?

A. Nathan Hale. A teacher who became a spy for General George Washington during the Revolutionary War, Hale was captured by British soldiers and hanged in 1776. No one knows for sure if the 21-year-old army captain actually spoke these exact words at the gallows, but it is believed he was familiar with the English writer Joseph Addison and was paraphrasing a line from the play *Cato*, "What pity is it/ That we can die but once to serve our country!" Nathan Hale is the official state hero of Connecticut.

Q. **Who were the five individuals in the "Committee of Five" appointed by the Continental-Confederation Congress to draft a statement declaring the colonists' reasons for wanting independence?**

A. John Adams of Massachusetts, Benjamin Franklin of Pennsylvania, Roger Sherman of Connecticut, Robert R. Livingston of New York, and Thomas Jefferson of Virginia. The committee subsequently asked Thomas Jefferson to write the Declaration of Independence.

Q. **Why does the American flag have stripes?**

A. The American flag is one of the most recognizable symbols of the United States, with its fifty white stars set against a blue field and its thirteen horizontal stripes of alternating red and white. Known variously as "Old Glory," "The Star-Spangled Banner," and "The Stars and Stripes," the U.S. flag has undergone a number of design changes over the course of American history. The stripes, however, have pretty much remained in place from the beginning.

Although it's unclear who originally designed the flag, evidence suggests it was Francis Hopkinson, a signer of the Declaration of Independence, in the late 1770s. Today, each of the flag's fifty stars represents a state. (The stars have accounted for most of the revisions to the flag, as the count had to be updated every time a new state joined the Union.) Originally, the stripes followed the same concept—each stripe was to represent a colony, and that number was thirteen when the nation was born.

The Flag Act, dated June 14, 1777, laid out the initial guidelines for flagmakers: "Resolved, that the flag of the United States be thirteen stripes, alternate red and white; that the union be thirteen stars, white in a blue field representing a new constellation."

In May of 1795, the numbers were changed to fifteen stars and fifteen stripes, but a later act, signed in 1818, established the format we have today—the flag would have no more than thirteen stripes, but a star would be added for each state in the Union.

Thank goodness for the limit on stripes. Imagine the consequences. The flag would either be three stories high or have stripes so thin that you'd need a magnifying glass to tell one from the other.

Q. Who were some notable Native Americans?

A. Let's face it; America's history is not exactly neat and tidy. When white settlers arrived in America, they realized they had a big problem—there were people already living there! The following figures represent the hundreds of tribal leaders who did everything they could to preserve the history and culture of their threatened people.

Tatanka Iyotaka, aka Sitting Bull: The principal chief of the Dakota Sioux was fierce, determined, and less than forgiving of the white miners who tried to take over the Black Hills in the late 1870s. Sitting Bull was born in 1831 and, while he earned a reputation for being ruthless in the Native American resistance efforts of his younger days, his big moment came in 1876. Trying to protect their land, Sitting Bull and his men defeated Custer's troops at the Battle of Little Bighorn. Sitting Bull then escaped to Canada. In 1881, he returned to America on the promise of a pardon, which he received. The legendary warrior then joined Buffalo Bill's Wild West Show, showcasing his riding skills and hunting prowess. But when he died at 69, Sitting Bull was still advising his people to hold on to their land and their heritage.

Tecumseh: While Tecumseh, a Shawnee chief, was no stranger to battle, he is more often recognized for his diplomatic efforts in the Native American plight. Born in Ohio in the late 1760s, Tecumseh was an impressive and charismatic orator. In 1809, when the Treaty of Fort Wayne signed over 2.5 million acres to the United States, Tecumseh was outraged. He tried to get all the Native American nations to join together, claiming that the land belonged to the people who were there first, and no one tribe could buy or sell any part of it. Tecumseh's hopes were to create solidarity among all native peoples, but the idea came too late. Eventually, Tecumseh joined forces with the British and was killed in battle in 1813.

Sequoyah: If it weren't for Sequoyah, a huge piece of Native American culture might be missing. Thanks to this Cherokee, born around 1766, the Cherokee language is not a mystery. Sequoyah created the syllabary, or syllable alphabet, for his people and taught the Cherokee how to read and write. The ability to communicate via the written word helped make the Cherokee Nation a leader among tribes everywhere. The giant sequoia tree is named after the man who felt that the pen would outlast the sword—and he was right. Sequoyah died in 1843 of natural causes.

John Ross: Though only one-eighth Cherokee, John Ross served as a chief in the Cherokee Nation from 1828 until his death in 1866. Over the years, Ross served as a translator for missionaries, a liaison between the Cherokee people and Washington politicians, and owned a farm (and slaves) in North Carolina. By the early 1820s, things did not look good for the Cherokee people. Ross took legal action to try to prevent the forced exile of the tribe. He was president of the Cherokee Constitutional Convention of 1827 and, for the next ten years, worked with the U.S. government and his people to seek assistance and justice for the Cherokee. Even though several court rulings found the Cherokee to be the rightful owners of land, they weren't enforced, and, slowly but surely, Ross's efforts went largely unrewarded. Ross is known for leading the Cherokee to Oklahoma in 1838 on what is commonly referred to as the "Trail of Tears."

Tashunca-uitco, aka Crazy Horse: At the tender age of 13, this legendary warrior was stealing horses from neighboring tribes. By the time he was 20, Crazy Horse was leading his first war party under the instruction of Chief Red Cloud. The Lakota warrior spent his life fighting for the preservation of his people's way of life. He amassed more than 1,200 warriors to help Sitting Bull defeat General Crook in 1876. After that, Sitting Bull and Crazy Horse joined forces, eventually defeating Custer at Little Bighorn. Crazy Horse continued to tirelessly defend his people's rights, but by 1877, there was little fight left in him. When trying to get to his sick wife, Crazy Horse was killed with a bayonet.

Hin-mah-too-yah-lat-kekt, aka Joseph the Younger:
Born in 1840 in what is now Oregon, Joseph the Younger (also called Chief Joseph) had some big shoes to fill. His father, Joseph the Elder, had converted to Christianity in 1838 in an attempt to make peace with white settlers. His father's efforts seemed to work, for his Nez Percé people were given land in Idaho. But in 1863, the U.S. government took the land back, and Joseph the Younger's father burned his Bible and his flag and refused to sign any new treaties. When Joseph succeeded his father as tribal chief in 1871, he clearly had to deal with a rather delicate situation. He eventually agreed to move his people to the now smaller reservation in Idaho, but never made it. They came under attack by white soldiers, fought back, and then dealt with the wrath of the government. In an impressive battle, 700 Native Americans fought 2,000 U.S. soldiers successfully until Joseph surrendered in 1877. He died in 1904 from what his doctor reported was a broken heart.

Makhpiya-Luta, aka Red Cloud: For most of his life, Red Cloud was fighting. At first, it was to defend his Oglala people against the Pawnee and Crow tribes, but by the time he reached his forties, Red Cloud was fighting the white man. His efforts led to the defeat of Fort Phil Kearny in Wyoming in 1867 and kept soldiers at bay (and in fear) for the rest of the winter. In the two years that followed, the government signed the Fort Laramie Treaty and gave the Native Americans land in Wyoming, Montana, and South Dakota. But soon after, the Black Hills were invaded, and Red Cloud and his people lost their land. Until his death in 1909, Red Cloud tried other ways to make peace and preserve the culture of his people, working with government officials and agents to reach a fair agreement.

Q. Who was Crispus Attucks, and how did he contribute to the revolutionaries' cause?

A. Attucks, the son of a Native American mother and an African father (and possibly a runaway slave), led the colonial protest that resulted in the Boston Massacre. His bold 1770 protest against the continuing influx of British troops to the Boston area turned into a rock-throwing riot against armed soldiers. Some of the British soldiers retaliated with gunfire, killing Attucks and four other colonists.

Q. Where did General George Cornwallis surrender to George Washington, effectively ending the American Revolution?

A. In Yorktown, Virginia. Cornwallis had retreated to coastal Virginia from North Carolina and waited to be resupplied. While the French navy closed off the sea route to British reinforcements, Washington arrived with his army from New York to trap Cornwallis against the seashore. After a siege lasting about three weeks (and which featured frequent artillery duels and trench raids), Cornwallis surrendered. At the Yorktown surrender ceremony, Cornwallis's subordinate tried to hand his sword to French General Comte Jean de Rochambeau. The French officer deferred the honor to his superior officer, General Washington.

Q. Where was the Continental Convention of 1787 held?

A. Philadelphia. Following the triumph of the Revolution, there remained the issue of what the country's new government would govern and how it would do so. A new constitution needed to be considered, so the Continental Convention of 1787 was held in Philadelphia.

Among the 55 delegates present were not-yet-president George Washington, Ben Franklin, Alexander Hamilton, and James Madison. Tossing the ineffective Articles of Confederation from 1781 into the wastebasket, they built a new and stronger form of government. The eventual result was the Constitution (and the accompanying Bill of Rights) and the basis of government structure and operation that still runs today.

Q. After the British burned down the Library of Congress in 1814, a new replacement collection was quickly made available. Where did it come from?

A. Monticello, Thomas Jefferson's home in Virginia. Thomas Jefferson sold his personal book collection, consisting of approximately 6,500 volumes, to the U.S. Congress.

Thomas Jefferson's home, Monticello, is a showplace of Jefferson's obsession with invention. During his time there, the house featured, among other new ideas,

automatic doors, a revolving bookstand, a primitive copy machine, and the modern dumbwaiter. But Jefferson's most famous invention was the Great Clock, an ingenious device that kept track of both the day and the time. It also struck an enormous gong on the roof of the main house hourly.

Thomas Jefferson appears on the nickel. On the back of that coin is his Monticello. In addition, Monticello also appears on the backside of certain $2 bills.

Q. What did Benjamin Franklin's epitaph say?

A. "The Body of B. Franklin Printer; Like the Cover of an old Book, Its Contents torn out, And stript of its Lettering and Gilding, Lies here, Food for Worms. But the Work shall not be wholly lost: For it will, as he believ'd, appear once more, In a new & more perfect Edition, Corrected and Amended By the Author."

Inventors

Q. Who invented barbed wire?

A. In 1915, Robert Frost gave the world the line "Good fences make good neighbors." But fences have often meant much more than that. To the brave men and women defending their property against the wilderness, they meant nothing less than safety and survival. But what makes a "good" fence?

In the American West, the answer was barbed wire— an invention that left its mark on an entire continent.

As America's settlers spread out into its vast heartland, they tried to take their fences with them. However, in comparison with the rock-strewn fields of New England or the lush pine forests of the South from whence they came, the pioneers found their new environs to be lacking in suitable material with which to build the barriers that would protect their land. At the time, it was the responsibility of landowners to keep roving animals out of their fields (rather than it being incumbent upon the owner of the animals to keep them controlled). As a result, farmers were left to deal with the problem of how to protect their crops in conjunction with the impossibility of building their traditional fences. A new solution simply had to be found. The answer came from the state of Illinois, which was on the border between the civilized East and the Wild West.

An Idea Whose Time Had Come

In 1873, a farmer named Henry Rose was desperate to control a "breachy" cow. His original idea was to attach a board covered with metallic points directly to the head of his cow. When the cow ran into a fence, the points would prick the cow and cause it to retreat. It came as a surprise to Rose (though probably not to anyone else) that requiring his cow to wear a plank all the time proved impractical. He then decided to attach the boards to his fence rather than to the cow. The solution seemed promising, and Rose proudly showed off his invention at a county fair where it caught the attention of a number of other inventors, including Joseph Glidden.

Joseph Glidden, working with a hand-cranked coffee mill in his kitchen, soon found that by twisting two lengths of wire together with a shorter piece in between to form a prickly barb, he could make a fence as effective as Rose's. He put up a test fence demonstrating his new invention, and word quickly spread. Isaac Ellwood, who had also seen Rose's display at the county fair and had been working on his own version, drove out to see Glidden's fence only to ride off in a rage when his wife commented that Glidden's barrier was superior to his. Ellwood was a shrewd businessman, however, and after he cooled down, he purchased an interest in Glidden's invention, and the two went into business together making barbed-wire fencing. Joseph Haish, also inspired by the Rose invention, introduced a rival barbed-wire fence around the same time.

All that was left was to convince a doubtful public that a few strands of thin wire could hold back determined cattle. The innumerable herds of Texas would be the proving ground, as barbed-wire salesmen threw up enclosures and invited ranchers to bring their most ornery cattle. To the amazement of the onlookers, barbed wire proved equal to the task again and again, and sales skyrocketed.

Don't Fence Me In

Ironically, even though barbed wire's most obvious use was to protect farmers' fields, it wasn't until the cattle ranchers seized on barbed wire that it began to transform the West. Large ranches quickly realized that by fencing off grazing land, they could effectively control the cattle industry, and miles of fencing sprang up across Texas and other territories. The fences weren't always well received. They injured cows and were sometimes put up without regard to traditional pasture or water rights. The winters of 1885 to 1887 were particularly brutal. Free-range cattle in northern ranges, accustomed to moving south in the face of impending blizzards, found their way blocked by the strange new fences. The cows froze to death by the thousands—carcasses stacked 400 yards deep against the fences in some places—in an event forever remembered as the Big Die-Up. Tempers naturally ran high, and there were open hostilities across the West, as armed factions cut down rival fences and put up new ones.

Despite the controversy, however, it proved impossible to reverse the trend to fence in land. Within about 25 years of the introduction of barbed wire, nearly all of what had previously been free-range land was fenced and under private ownership. The open land of the West, at one time considered an inexhaustible resource for all to use, was divided up and made off limits to the general public. The new invention channeled people into fixed paths of transit centered around railroads and towns. These patterns evolved into the interstate highways and cities we know today. It's no exaggeration to say that barbed wire is responsible for the shape of the modern West as we see it today—and it can all be traced back to Henry Rose's breachy cow.

Q. What 1793 invention dramatically transformed the American South?

A. Eli Whitney's cotton gin removed the seeds from cotton and made mass production of the South's cotton possible—and thus cotton production more profitable. Southern cotton plantations were soon shipping massive amounts of cotton to New England and Europe.

Eli Whitney said he came up with the idea for the cotton gin as he observed a cat trying to pull a chicken through a fence. Whitney took note of the fact that the cat was successful only at pulling a few feathers through the fence.

Q. What important stuff have women invented?

A. If you think men have the market cornered on inventions, think again. It turns out that the fairer sex is responsible for some of history's most notable breakthroughs.

Women came up with ideas and specifications for such useful items as life rafts (Maria Beasley), circular saws (Tabitha Babbitt), medical syringes (Letitia Geer), and underwater lamps and telescopes (Sarah Mather). Giuliana Tesoro was a prolific inventor in the textile industry; flame-resistant fibers and permanent-press properties are among her many contributions. The Tesoro Corporation holds more than 125 of her textile-related patents.

Not surprisingly, some well-known inventions by women are associated with the home. In 1930, for example, dietician Ruth Wakefield and her husband Kenneth were operating a tourist lodge near Boston. While mixing a batch of cookies for guests one day, Ruth discovered she had run out of baker's chocolate. In a rush to come up with something, Wakefield substituted broken pieces of Nestlé semi-sweet chocolate. She expected them to melt into the dough to create chocolate cookies; they didn't, and the surprising result was the chocolate chip cookie.

In the late 1950s, Ruth Handler drew inspiration from watching her daughter and her daughter's friends play with paper dolls. After noticing that the girls used the dolls to act out future events rather than those in the present, Handler set out to create a grown-up, three-dimensional doll. She even endowed it with breasts. Handler named her creation after her daughter, and the Barbie doll was introduced in 1959. Handler, incidentally, was one of the founders of the toy giant Mattel.

Of course, not all female inventors have been interested in cookies and dolls. Consider Mary Anderson. While taking a trip from Alabama to New York City just after the turn of the 20th century, she noticed that when it rained, drivers had to open their car windows to see. Anderson invented a swinging-arm device with a rubber blade that the driver operated by using a lever. In 1903, she received a patent for what became known as the windshield wiper; by 1916, it was standard on most vehicles.

Movie actress Hedy Lamarr's invention was a matter of national security. Lamarr, born Hedwig Eva Maria Kiesler in Austria, emigrated to the United States in the 1930s. In addition to leading the glamorous life of a film star, she became a pioneer in the field of wireless communication.

Lamarr and composer George Anthiel developed a secret communications system to help the Allies in World War II—their method of manipulating radio frequencies was used to create unbreakable codes. The invention proved invaluable again two decades later when it was used aboard naval vessels during the Cuban Missile Crisis.

Q. What vegetable-based toy started an empire in Rhode Island?

A. Mr. Potato Head. In the late 1940s, George Lerner had the idea to create plastic mouths, eyes, and noses that could be pushed into pieces of produce to make funny faces. Toy companies pooh-poohed the idea, but in 1951, Lerner met with a small family-owned company of Rhode Island toymakers, Hassenfeld Brothers, that sold school supplies and was trying to move into the toy market. The Hassenfelds loved Lerner's idea, and on April 30, 1952, the Mr. Potato Head Funny Face kit debuted, selling for just under a dollar. As the first toy advertised on TV, it became an instant success, with sales hitting more than $4 million in the first year. That gave Hassenfeld Brothers all the basis it needed to break into the toy market. They also streamlined the company name for their new image, rebranding themselves as Hasbro.

Q. Who developed the birth control pill?

A. Before 1960, activist Margaret Sanger dreamt of a "magic pill" for birth control that women could take as easily as an aspirin. This dream became a reality, thanks to Sanger and a few well-placed friends.

In the 1950s, as American women were having babies in unprecedented numbers. A big family was the perceived ideal. However, many women longed for an inexpensive, reliable, and simple form of contraception. Diaphragms were costly. Condoms and other contraceptives were unreliable. None were easy to use.

Fortunately, history brought together Margaret Sanger, Katharine McCormick, Gregory Pincus, and John Rock.

The Players
Born in 1879, Margaret Sanger was 19 when her mother, who had given birth to 11 children and suffered 7 miscarriages, died from tuberculosis. In 1916, as a nurse in New York treating poor women recovering from botched illegal abortions, Sanger began defying the law by distributing contraceptives. In 1921, she founded the American Birth Control League, a precursor to the Planned Parenthood Federation, and in 1923 opened the first legal birth control clinic in the United States. For the next 30 years, Sanger advocated for safe and effective birth control while dreaming of a "magic pill" that would usher in an era of female-controlled contraception.

Katharine Dexter McCormick was born into a prominent Chicago family in 1875. In 1904, she married Stanley McCormick, heir to the International Harvester Corporation fortune. McCormick's life changed when her husband developed schizophrenia. Believing the condition to be hereditary, McCormick vowed to remain childless. In 1917, she met Sanger at a suffragette rally and took up her cause. Following her husband's death in 1947, McCormick dedicated his $15 million estate to the discovery of Sanger's "magic pill."

In January 1951, Sanger met Dr. Gregory Pincus, a once-heralded biologist at Harvard University who was vilified as "Dr. Frankenstein" after developing in-vitro fertilization in rabbits in 1934. Booted from Harvard, Pincus was working in obscurity at a Clark University lab when he met Sanger. He told Sanger her "magic pill" was possible by using hormones as a contraceptive. Sanger quickly arranged a grant from Planned Parenthood for Pincus to research the use of progesterone in inhibiting ovulation and preventing pregnancy. Within a year, Pincus confirmed that the drug was effective in lab animals.

A Bitter Pill

Pincus next set out to invent a progesterone pill, unaware that both Syntex and G.D. Searle pharmaceutical companies had already achieved it. (Neither company pursued its use as an oral contraceptive for fear of a public backlash.) Worse for Pincus, Planned Parenthood halted its funding, saying his research was too risky.

In late 1952, following a chance encounter with Dr. John Rock, a renowned fertility expert and birth control advocate from Harvard. Rock was a devout Catholic who reconciled the Vatican's rigid stance against artificial birth control with his personal conviction that planned parenting and contraception promoted healthy marriages. Rock floored Pincus when he explained that his tests using progesterone injections on female patients (ironically, attempting to stimulate pregnancy) worked as a contraceptive.

A New Era

Then in June 1953, Sanger introduced Pincus to McCormick. Sold on Pincus's research, McCormick cut him a check for $40,000 to restart the pill project. Pincus recruited Rock, and in 1954, using progesterone pills provided by G.D. Searle, they conducted the first human trials of the drug with 50 women, successfully establishing the 21-day administering cycle still used today.

In May 1960, Searle received FDA approval to sell the progesterone pill, Enovid, for birth control purposes. Within five years, six million American women were using the "magic pill."

Q. Did Benjamin Franklin discover electricity?

A. As it turns out, Benjamin Franklin did not discover electricity. What's more, the kite he famously flew in 1752 while conducting an experiment was not struck by lightning. If it had been, Franklin would be remembered as a colonial publisher and assemblyman killed by his own curiosity.

Before Ben

Blessed with one of the keenest minds in history, Benjamin Franklin was a scientific genius who made groundbreaking discoveries in the basic nature and properties of electricity. Electrical science, however, dates to 1600, when Dr. William Gilbert, physician to Queen Elizabeth, published a treatise about his research on electricity and magnetism. European inventors who later expanded on Gilbert's knowledge included Otto von Guericke of Germany, Charles Francois Du Fay of France, and Stephen Gray of England.

The Science of Electricity

Franklin became fascinated with electricity after seeing a demonstration by an itinerant showman (and doctor) named Archibald Spencer in Boston in 1743. Two years later, he bought a Leyden jar—a contraption invented by a Dutch scientist that used a glass container wrapped in foil to create a crude battery. Other researchers had demonstrated the properties of the device, and Franklin set about to increase its capacity to generate electricity while testing his own scientific hypotheses. Among the principles he established was the conservation of charge, one of the most important laws of physics. In a paper published in 1750, he announced the discovery of the induced charge and broadly outlined the existence of the electron. His experiments led him to coin many of the terms currently used in the science of electricity, such as battery, conductor, condenser, charge, discharge, uncharged, negative, minus, plus, electric shock, and electrician.

As Franklin came to understand the nature of electricity, he began to theorize about the electrical nature of lightning. In 1751, he outlined in a British scientific journal his idea for an experiment that involved placing a long metal rod on a high tower or steeple to draw an electric charge from passing thunder clouds, which would throw off visible electric sparks. A year later, French scientist Georges-Louis Leclerc successfully conducted such an experiment.

The Kite Runner

Franklin had not heard of Leclerc's success when he undertook his own experiment in June 1752. Instead of a church spire, he affixed his kite to a sharp, pointed wire. To the end of his kite string he tied a key, and to the key a ribbon made of silk (for insulation). While flying his kite on a cloudy day as a thunderstorm approached, Franklin noticed that loose threads on the kite string stood erect, as if they had been suspended from a common conductor. The key sparked when he touched it, showing it was charged with electricity. But had the kite actually been struck by lightning, Franklin would likely have been killed, as was Professor Georg Wilhelm Richmann of St. Petersburg, Russia, when he attempted the same experiment a few months later.

The Lightning Rod

Although Franklin did not discover electricity, he did uncover many of its fundamental principles and proved that lightning is, in fact, electricity. He used his knowledge to create the lightning rod, an invention that today protects land structures and ships at sea. He never patented the lightning rod but instead generously promoted it as a boon to humankind. In 21st-century classrooms, the lightning rod is still cited as a classic example of the way fundamental science can produce practical inventions.

Q. When was JELL-O invented?

A. JELL-O dates back to 1845, when Peter Cooper obtained a patent for a flavorless gelatin dessert. Cooper packaged the product in convenient boxes—complete with instructions—but did little to promote it. In the 1890s, Pearl B. Wait perfected a fruit-flavored version of Cooper's gelatin dessert. In 1899, Wait sold the business to his neighbor and owner of the Genesee Pure Food Company, Orator Frank Woodward. A savvy promoter, Woodward began advertising JELL-O in such magazines as *Ladies' Home Journal*, calling it "America's Most Famous Dessert." Sales soared, and they have never really waned.

Q. What 1902 invention greatly improved the quality of life throughout the world?

A. When Willis Carrier built the first effective air-conditioning unit in 1902, his goal was not to cool the room to make it comfortable for human beings. Rather, he was trying to prevent paper from contracting and expanding in hot and humid conditions. The grateful recipient of the air-conditioning system was Sackett-Wilhelms Lithographing & Publishing Company of Brooklyn, New York. The first commercial use of air-conditioning to make people more comfortable came 15 years later.

Q. If Al Gore didn't invent the Internet, who did?

A. When the Internet was conceived in the 1960s, other matters, such as getting to know his future wife, Tipper, at their senior prom, consumed Al Gore. But Gore wasn't completely full of you-know-what when some years later he claimed to have taken "the initiative in creating the Internet." As a congressman, he helped popularize the term "information superhighway" and sponsored a number of bills that aided in forming the Internet as we know it today.

But we digress. The best candidate to credit with the invention of the most expansive and influential technology of our time is Robert Taylor. Born in 1932, Taylor was trained as an experimental psychologist and mathematician, and he worked for defense contractor Martin Marietta early in his career. Under J. C. R. Licklider (who is now known as computing's Johnny Appleseed), Taylor went to work in the Department of Defense's information processing office in the 1960s.

Back then, communication between several computers was akin to communication via telegraph—only one machine could talk to another at a time. At the Department of Defense, Taylor had three computers at his disposal: one connected to the System Development Corporation in Santa Monica, California; one for Project Genie at the University of California-Berkeley; and one hooked into the Compatible Time-Sharing System at MIT. The problem? To talk to the computer at MIT, Taylor had to be sitting at the Defense department's MIT-designated computer. To talk to the System Development Corporation in Santa Monica, he had to be on that designated computer. And so on.

Tired of walking from terminal to terminal, Taylor spared us from having hundreds of laptops in our offices by sensing the need for "interactive computing," or one computer terminal that would connect with all others. He and Licklider coauthored the landmark paper "The Computer as a Communication Device," which was published in *Science and Technology* in April 1968.

By the end of the decade, Taylor had spearheaded the creation of the ARPANET (Advanced Research Projects Agency Network), which featured newly developed packet -switching technology (using a communication line to connect to more than one other computer at a time) and was the precursor to the Internet. Today, the entire civilized world has jumped on board and, to borrow Gore's catchphrase, is rolling down the "information superhighway."

Politics and Government

Q. What was the Presidential Succession
Act of 1947?

A. It's common knowledge that if the president of
the United States dies or is removed from office,
the vice president takes over. But what happens if the
VP is unavailable? President Harry Truman signed into
law the Presidential Succession Act of 1947, placing the
Speaker of the House second in line for the presidency
and creating the following order of successors to the
White House.

1. Vice President
2. Speaker of the House of Representatives
3. President Pro Tempore of the Senate
4. Secretary of State
5. Secretary of the Treasury
6. Secretary of Defense
7. Attorney General
8. Secretary of the Interior
9. Secretary of Agriculture
10. Secretary of Commerce
11. Secretary of Labor
12. Secretary of Health and Human Services
13. Secretary of Housing and Urban Development
14. Secretary of Transportation
15. Secretary of Energy
16. Secretary of Education
17. Secretary of Veterans Affairs

Q. What was the Chappaquiddick scandal?

A. Since being elected to the Senate in 1962, Edward M. "Ted" Kennedy had been known as a liberal who championed causes such as education and health care, but he had less success in his personal life. On July 18, 1969, Kennedy attended a party on Chappaquiddick Island in Massachusetts. He left the party with 29-year-old Mary Jo Kopechne, who had campaigned for Ted's late brother Robert. Soon after the two left the party, Kennedy's car veered off a bridge and Kopechne drowned. An experienced swimmer, Kennedy said he tried to rescue her but the tide was too strong. He swam to shore, went back to the party, and returned with two other men. Their rescue efforts also failed, but Kennedy waited until the next day to report the accident, calling his lawyer and Kopechne's parents first, claiming the crash had dazed him. There was speculation that he tried to cover up that he was driving under the influence, but nothing was ever proven. Kennedy pleaded guilty to leaving the scene of an accident, received a two-month suspended jail sentence, and lost his driver's license for a year. The scandal may have contributed to his failed presidential bid in 1980, but it didn't hurt his reputation in the Senate. In April 2006, *Time* magazine named him one of "America's 10 Best Senators."

Q. How did American women get the right to vote?

A. Between 1818 and 1820, Fanny Wright, a feminist from Scotland, lectured throughout the United States on such topics as voting rights for women, birth control, and equality between the sexes in education and marriage laws. Little did she know that it would take another 100 years for American women to achieve the right to vote on these issues.

To be technical, Margaret Brent, a landowner in Maryland, was the very first woman in the United States to call for voting rights. In 1647, Brent insisted on two votes in the colonial assembly—one for herself and one for the man for whom she held power of attorney. The governor rejected her request.

Then there was Abigail Adams. In 1776, she wrote to her husband, John, asking him to remember the ladies in the new code of laws he was drafting. She was summarily dismissed.

Almost half a century later, Fanny Wright showed up from Scotland. Although she recognized the gender inequities in the United States, she still fell in love with the country and became a naturalized citizen in 1825.

It wasn't until the 1840s, however, that the feminist ball really got rolling. Because progress was achieved in fits and spurts, women's suffrage eventually took the good part of a century after that to come to fruition.

Before the Civil War, the women's suffrage movement and abolition organizations focused on many of the same issues. The two movements were closely linked in action and deed, specifically at the World Anti-Slavery Convention in London in 1840. However, female delegates to the convention, among them Lucretia Mott and Elizabeth Cady Stanton, were not allowed to participate in the activities because of their gender. London is a long way to travel to sit in the back of a room and be silent. Stanton and Mott resolved to organize a convention to discuss the rights of women.

The convention was finally held in 1848 in Seneca Falls, New York. Stanton presented her *Declaration of Sentiments*, the first formal action by women in the United States to advocate civil rights and suffrage.

Two groups formed at the end of the 1860s—the National Woman Suffrage Association (NWSA) and the American Woman Suffrage Association (AWSA). The NWSA, led by Susan B. Anthony and Stanton, worked to change voting laws on the federal level by way of an amendment to the U.S. Constitution. The AWSA, led by Lucy Stone and Julia Ward Howe, worked to change the laws on the state level. The two groups were united in 1890 and renamed the National American Woman Suffrage Association.

In 1916, Alice Paul formed the National Woman's Party (NWP). Based on the idea that action, not words, would achieve the suffragists' mission, the NWP staged Silent Sentinels outside the White House during which NWP members held banners and signs that goaded the president. When World War I came along, many assumed the Silent Sentinels would end. Instead, the protesters incorporated the current events into their messages and were ultimately arrested. Once the public got wind of the horrendous treatment the women were subjected to in jail, the public tide turned in their favor. In 1917, President Woodrow Wilson announced his support for a suffrage amendment. In the summer of 1920, Tennessee ratified the Nineteenth Amendment—the 36th state to do so—and in August of that year, women gained the right to vote. It had certainly been a long time coming.

Q. What was the Iran-Contra Affair?

A. On July 8, 1985, President Ronald Reagan told the American Bar Association that Iran was part of a "confederation of terrorist states." He failed to mention that members of his administration were secretly planning to sell weapons to Iran to facilitate the release of U.S. hostages held in Lebanon by pro-Iranian terrorist groups. Profits from the arms sales were secretly sent to Nicaragua to aid rebel forces, known as the contras, in their attempt to overthrow the country's democratically elected government. The incident became known as the Iran-Contra Affair and was the biggest scandal of Reagan's administration. The weapons sale to Iran was authorized by Robert McFarlane, head of the National Security Council (NSC), in violation of U.S. government policies regarding terrorists and military aid to Iran. NSC staff member Oliver North arranged for a portion of the $48 million paid by Iran to be sent to the contras, which violated a 1984 law banning this type of aid. North and his secretary Fawn Hall also shredded critical documents. President Reagan repeatedly denied rumors that the United States had exchanged arms for hostages, but later stated that he'd been misinformed. He created a Special Review Board to investigate. In February 1987, the board found the president not guilty. Others involved were found guilty but either had their sentences overturned on appeal or were later pardoned by George H. W. Bush.

Q. Who holds the record for the longest filibuster in Congress?

A. Senator Strom Thurmond conducted the longest filibuster ever on August 29, 1957. He spoke nonstop for 24 hours and 18 minutes in opposition to the Civil Rights Act of 1957. However, the bill passed two hours after he failed to convince any senators to change their vote on the bill.

Q. Who was the longest-serving member in congressional history?

A. Robert Byrd. He earned the record on November 18, 2009, with 56 years and 320 days of combined service in the House and Senate. He also holds the record for longest unbroken tenure, another impressive feat. He began his service as a U.S. representative in 1953 and became a senator in 1959, where he served until his death in 2010.

Q. Why are Democrats on the left and Republicans on the right?

A. In this era of cable-channel charlatans, jingoist radio shows, and boorish bloggers, it's tempting to see things in black and white. In political discourse, this polarization finds expression in the  terms "left" and "right." Regardless of what their respective defenders and detractors might like to believe, "right" in this sense isn't a synonym for "correct." And "left" doesn't conjure up the bogeyman—even if our word "sinister" does come from *sinestra si*, Latin for "left."

The concept of the political "left" and "right" can be traced across the Atlantic Ocean to France. It came to the fore in 1789 during the French Revolution, when the National Assembly first convened. The Assembly consisted of three groups, known as "estates." The first estate was the clergy, the second the nobility, and the third the commoners. (The term "fourth estate," which is used to describe journalism, has its roots here.)

These estates did not get along particularly well. During meetings, the first and second estates began to congregate on the right side of the chamber; the third estate tended to sit on the left. This ad hoc arrangement became the norm over the course of the Revolution.

As one might expect, the clergy and nobility—the right— were pretty happy with the way things were. They were conservative toward change to the status quo. By contrast, the commoners—the left—were tired of suffering at the hands of the wealthy. They were liberal toward change.

This ideological bifurcation was brought to the English-speaking world's attention in Thomas Carlyle's popular 1837 treatise on the French Revolution. Political pundits in Britain soon adopted it, even though Parliament had no such seating chart.

During the 19th century, the concept of a political right and left moved across the pond to America. It became shorthand for the conservatism we ascribe to Republicans and the liberalism with which we characterize Democrats.

The reality, of course, is more nuanced, but broadcast blowhards work best in black and white.

Q. Who were the Keating Five?

A. After the banking industry was deregulated in the 1980s, savings and loan banks were allowed to invest deposits in commercial real estate, not just residential. Many savings banks began making risky investments, and the Federal Home Loan Bank Board (FHLBB) tried to stop them, against the wishes of the Reagan administration, which was against government interference with business. In 1989, when the Lincoln Savings and Loan Association of Irvine, California, collapsed, its chairman, Charles H. Keating Jr., accused the FHLBB and its former head Edwin J. Gray of conspiring against him. Gray testified that five senators had asked him to back off on the Lincoln investigation. These senators—Alan Cranston of California, Dennis DeConcini of Arizona, John Glenn of Ohio, Donald Riegle of Michigan, and John McCain of Arizona—became known as the Keating Five after it was revealed that they received a total of $1.3 million in campaign contributions from Keating. While an investigation determined that all five acted improperly, they all claimed this was a standard campaign funding practice. In August 1991, the Senate Ethics Committee recommended censure for Cranston and criticized the other four for "questionable conduct." Cranston had already decided not to run for reelection in 1992. DeConcini and Riegle served out their terms but did not run for reelection in 1994. John Glenn was reelected in 1992 and served until he retired in 1999. John McCain continues his work in the Senate.

Q. Which Supreme Court decision established the "separate but equal" doctrine?

A. *Plessy v. Ferguson*. In 1892, Homer Plessy (who traced some of his ancestors back to the French, Spanish, and Caribbean settlers of Louisiana and was therefore considered "colored") sat in the "White" car of the East Louisiana Railroad and was arrested for doing so. Plessy's case went all the way to the U.S. Supreme Court, where his lawyers maintained that the requirement to sit in a "Colored" car violated Plessy's rights under the Thirteenth and Fourteenth Amendments. (The Thirteenth Amendment abolished slavery. The Fourteenth Amendment granted citizenship to "all persons born or naturalized in the United States," which included former slaves; it also forbade states from denying any person within their jurisdictions "the equal protection of any laws.") The Supreme Court upheld Louisiana's segregation statute.

The 1954 Supreme Court case *Brown v. Board of Education* unanimously overturned the *Plessy v. Ferguson* decision that established the "separate but equal" doctrine. The justices ruling on *Brown* decided that segregation laws violated the equal protection clause of the Fourteenth Amendment. Justice Stanley Reed, the last living member of this court, died at age 95 on April 2, 1980. After retiring from the court in 1957, Reed served on President Dwight D. Eisenhower's Civil Rights Commission.

Q. Rosa Parks refused to give up her seat on a bus in what Southern city?

A. Montgomery, Alabama. On December 1, 1955, Rosa Parks, a 42-year-old African American woman, was on her way home from work when she deliberately broke the state's segregation law by refusing to yield her seat on a bus to a standing white passenger. Parks was arrested and was later found guilty, receiving a fine and a suspended sentence. Her action sparked a successful, yearlong boycott of the Montgomery bus system by the black community led by a young preacher named Martin Luther King Jr. This event is generally credited as the birth of the modern U.S. civil rights movement.

Q. Where did the Republican Party begin?

A. A number of towns claim to be the birthplace of the Republican Party. Exeter, New Hampshire, has the earliest claim, pointing to a meeting of abolitionists called by Amos Tuck in 1853 at Major Blake's Hotel (aka the Squamscott Hotel) in which the formation of an anti-slavery "Republican Party" was discussed. Unfortunately, no action seems to have been taken following this meeting, and the Republican Party wasn't officially established in New Hampshire for another couple of years. Crawfordsville, Iowa, takes the next claim chronologically, arguing that defectors from the Whig Party met in private at Seceder Church there in February 1854 to plan a new party. A month after that, what is sometimes considered the first public meeting of proto-Republicans was held at the Little White Schoolhouse in Ripon, Wisconsin. Finally, the first official party meeting, a statewide convention that created a party platform and nominated candidates for office, took place outdoors in Jackson, Michigan, on July 6, 1854.

Q. **Which city hosted the 1968 Democratic National Convention?**

A. Chicago. The 1968 Democratic National Convention was perhaps more memorable for what happened outside the convention hall than what happened inside, as youthful protesters fought police in the streets. With the nation divided by the Vietnam War and the assassinations of Martin Luther King Jr. and Robert F. Kennedy fueling animosity, the city became a battleground for antiwar protests. Confrontations between protesters and police turned violent, and Americans witnessed it all on national television.

Q. **What was the Teapot Dome scandal?**

A. The Teapot Dome Scandal was the largest of numerous scandals during the presidency of Warren Harding. Teapot Dome is an oil field reserved for emergency use by the U.S. Navy located on public land in Wyoming. Oil companies and politicians claimed the reserves were not necessary and that the oil companies could supply the navy in the event of shortages. In 1922, Interior Secretary Albert B. Fall accepted $404,000 in illegal gifts from oil company executives in return for leasing the rights to the oil at Teapot Dome to Mammoth Oil without asking for competitive bids. The leases were legal but the gifts were not. Fall's attempts to keep the gifts secret failed, and, on April 14, 1922, *The Wall Street Journal* exposed the bribes. Fall denied the charges, but an investigation revealed a $100,000 no-interest loan in return for leases that Fall had forgotten to cover up. In 1927, the Supreme Court ruled that the oil leases had been illegally obtained, and the U.S. Navy regained control of Teapot Dome and other reserves. Fall was found guilty of bribery in 1929, fined $100,000, and sentenced to one year in prison. He was the first cabinet member imprisoned for his actions while in office. President Harding was not aware of the scandal at the time of his death in 1923, but it contributed to his administration being considered one of the most corrupt in history.

Q. Do Social Security numbers contain a secret code?

A. Yes, but as secret codes go, it's duller than dirt. It's also not very secret.

Social Security numbers have nine digits. The first three digits reveal the geographic area of the holder—or at least the geographic area in which the holder lived when he or she applied for the Social Security number. The digits start low on the East Coast and get higher as you move west. For example, a Social Security number starting with 648 indicates a card issued in New Mexico.

This part of the code was designed in the mid-1930s, when Social Security numbers were doled out by individual states. After a state issued a card, the holder's information was sent for filing at the main Social Security office in Baltimore. This was long before computers, so the geographic coding helped if someone wanted to look up a Social Security number.

Assignment of the middle two numbers is confusing, so let's first address the final four numbers. They are four digits that range from 0001 to 9999.

Now for those pesky middle numbers. In each state, the first 9,999 people are issued cards with middle numbers 01, followed by a four-number sequence mentioned above that ranges from 0001 to 9999. It would seem that after the 01s are exhausted, starting with the 10,000th person, the middle two numbers would be 02. Wrong. After the 01s, the middle numbers assigned are, in order, 03, 05, 07, and 09.

After the 09 numbers are exhausted, the middle numbers become 10, followed by even-numbered middle digits up through 98. After all the Social Security numbers that include those middle two digits have been issued, the middle-number sequence goes to 02 through 08. Then comes 11, followed by all the odd numbers up to 99.

Get the feeling people running the Social Security Administration had too much time on their hands? Thankfully, the final four numbers get assigned consecutively as applications for cards roll in—no trick there. And neither Social Security cards nor Social Security numbers are coded to reveal race or other demographic information.

The numbering system may be cumbersome, but it can reveal a bogus Social Security number. For example, those who apply for a card in New Hampshire might get a number starting with 001, followed by odd-numbered middle digits. Most of the even-numbered middle digits have not yet been used, so if a number like 001-96-1234 appears on a Social Security card, that card is a fake.

Money and Business

Q. Why is there a pyramid with an eye on the dollar bill?

A. That trippy image on the dollar bill—the one of an unfinished pyramid with an eye hovering over it—seems better suited for a Pink Floyd album cover than U.S. legal tender. Well, there's a method to the madness, and we're here to tell you what it is.

The pyramid, along with its counterpart on the other end of the back of the dollar—the eagle grasping an olive branch and arrows in its talons—are the two sides of the Great Seal of the United States. They've been part of the bill's design since 1935.

While the country was still in its nascent stages, the Continental Congress conscripted three of the architects of the Declaration of Independence—Benjamin Franklin, Thomas Jefferson, and John Adams—to create a seal for the United States that would be used as a coat of arms. In typical bureaucratic fashion, the process took six years and two more committees to complete.

The intent was to capture all of the ideals of the new nation in one graphic image. Naturally, different patriots had different ideas about how this image should look, but they all wanted it to convey the notion of freedom and the revolutionary nature of the country's birth. A close look at the pyramid on the dollar might make you think that Mr. Franklin took one too many lightning bolts to the head, but every aspect of the seal has a precise meaning.

Actually, Franklin's committee didn't even suggest the pyramid—only the eye that floats above it. The pyramid was the result of a collaborative effort, but it did, nonetheless, make the intended statement. The pyramid itself has thirteen layers, symbolizing, of course, the thirteen original colonies. At the base of the pyramid is the year 1776 in Roman numerals.

The pyramid is believed to symbolize strength and durability. Its unfinished state suggests that America will always be a work in progress, striving for greatness. The eye hovering over the pyramid is the "Eye of Providence," a classic symbol that connotes divine guidance. The Latin phrase *Annuit Coeptis* (He Has Favored Our Undertakings) is above the pyramid. Underneath it is another Latin phrase, *Novus Ordo Seclorum* (A New Order of the Ages).

There you have it. The unfinished pyramid with an eye really does have a purpose on the dollar bill, though it would still look cool on a Pink Floyd album cover.

Q. Was history's first recorded billionaire a high school dropout?

A. Yes. John D. Rockefeller Sr., history's first billionaire, dropped out two months before his high school graduation to take business courses at Folsom Mercantile College. Rockefeller founded the Standard Oil Company in 1870, made his billions before the company was broken up by the government for being a monopoly, and spent his last 40 years giving away his riches, primarily to causes related to health and education.

Q. Which are the most rare and valuable U.S. coins?

A. Why are certain coins so valuable? Some simply have very low mintages, and some are error coins. In some cases (with gold, in particular), most of the pieces were confiscated and melted. Better condition always adds value.

The current mints and marks are Philadelphia (P, or no mark), Denver (D), and San Francisco (S). Mints in Carson City, Nevada (CC); Dahlonega, Georgia (D); and New Orleans (O) shut down long ago, which adds appeal to their surviving coinage. Here are the most prized and/or interesting U.S. coins, along with an idea of what they're worth:

1787 Brasher gold doubloon: It was privately minted by goldsmith Ephraim Brasher before the U.S. Mint's founding in 1793. The coin was slightly lighter than a $5 gold piece, and at one point in the 1970s it was the most expensive U.S. coin ever sold. Seven known; last sold for $625,000.

1792 half-disme (5¢ piece): Disme was the old terminology for "dime," so half a disme was five cents. George Washington supposedly provided the silver for this mintage. Was Martha the model for Liberty's image? If so, her hairdo suggests she'd been helping Ben Franklin with electricity experiments. Perhaps 1,500 minted; sells for up to $1.3 million.

1804 silver dollar: Though actually minted in 1834 and later, the official mint delivery figure of 19,570 refers to the 1804 issue. Watch out—counterfeits abound. Only 15 known; worth up to $4.1 million.

1849 Coronet $20 gold piece: How do you assess a unique coin's value? The Smithsonian owns the only authenticated example, the very first gold "double eagle." Why mint only one? It was a trial strike of the new series. Rumors persist of a second trial strike that ended up in private hands. If true, it hasn't surfaced in more than 150 years. Never sold; literally priceless.

1870-S $3 gold piece: Apparently, only one (currently in private hands) was struck, though there are tales of a second one placed in the cornerstone of the then-new San Francisco Mint building (now being renovated as a museum). If the building is ever demolished, don't expect to see it imploded. One known; estimated at $1.2 million.

1876-CC 20-cent piece: Remember when everyone confused the new Susan B. Anthony dollars with quarters? That's what comes of ignoring history. A century before, this 20-cent coin's resemblance to the quarter caused similar frustration. Some 18 known; up to $175,000.

1894-S Barber dime: The Barber designs tended to wear quickly, so any Barber coin in great condition is scarce enough. According to his daughter Hallie, San Francisco Mint director John Daggett struck two-dozen 1894-S coins, mostly as gifts for his rich banker pals. Dad gave little Hallie three of the dimes, and she used one to buy herself the costliest ice cream in history. Twenty-four minted, ten known; as high as $1.3 million.

1907 MCMVII St. Gaudens $20 gold piece: This is often considered the loveliest U.S. coin series ever. Its debut featured the year in Roman numerals, unique in U.S. coinage. The first, ultra-high-relief version was stunning in its clarity and beauty, but it proved too time-consuming to mint, so a less striking (but still impressive) version became the standard. About 11,000 minted, but very few in ultra-high relief; those have sold for $1.5 million.

1909-S VDB Lincoln cent: It's a favorite among collectors, though not vanishingly rare. Only about a fourth of Lincoln pennies from the series' kickoff year featured designer Victor D. Brenner's initials on the reverse; even now, an occasional "SVDB" will show up in change. There were 484,000 minted; worth up to $7,500.

1913 Liberty Head nickel: This coin wasn't supposed to be minted. The Mint manufactured the dies as a contingency before the Buffalo design was selected for 1913. Apparently, Mint employee Samuel W. Brown may have known that the Liberty dies were slated for destruction and therefore minted five of these for his personal gain. One of the most prized U.S. coins—and priced accordingly at $1.8 million.

1913-S Barber quarter: Forty thousand of these were made—the lowest regular-issue mintage of the 20th century. Some Barbers wore so flat that the head on the obverse was reduced to a simple outline. Quite rare in good condition; can bring up to $24,000.

1915 Panama-Pacific $50 gold piece: This large commemorative piece was offered in both octagonal and round designs. Approximately 1,100 were minted; prices range from $40,000 to $155,000.

1916 Liberty Standing quarter: This coin depicts a wardrobe malfunction . . . except by design! Many were shocked when the new coin displayed Lady Liberty's bared breast. By mid-1917, she was donning chain mail. Like the Barber quarter before it, the Liberty Standing wore out rapidly. With only 52,000 minted in 1916, the series' inaugural year, a nice specimen will set you back nearly $40,000.

1933 St. Gaudens $20 gold piece: This coin is an outlaw. All of the Saint's final mintage were to be melted down—and most were. Only one specific example is legal to own; other surviving 1933 Saints remain hidden from the threat of Treasury confiscation. The legal one sold in 2002 for an incredible $7.6 million.

1937-D "three-legged" Buffalo nickel: A new employee at the Denver Mint tried polishing some damage off a die with an emery stick. He accidentally ground the bison's foreleg off, leaving a disembodied hoof. No telling exactly how many were struck, but they sure look funny. Up to $30,000.

1943 bronze Lincoln cent: This was the exciting year of the steel penny—except someone flubbed and minted a few on standard bronze planchets (coin blanks) left over from 1942. Surely the dozen known examples can't be all that exist—you might find this one in your pocket! A bronze Lincoln cent sold for $112,500 in 2000.

Q. How did the Walt Disney Company control what businesses could open in the area around Walt Disney World in Orlando, Florida?

A. It bought about 27,000 acres' of land around the area. Walt Disney had been disappointed in how the area around Disneyland in California had been developed, so he made sure that he and his company would have a voice in what was built around the Florida theme park. Although Disney died in 1966, his brother Roy Disney saw the project through to fruition. Walt Disney World, consisting at the time of only the Magic Kingdom and two hotels, opened to the public in 1971.

Q. In 1970 this area in Northern California was still called Valley of the Heart's Delight. By what name is it better known today?

A. Silicon Valley. Fertile orchards that had once made this an agricultural area inspired the original name. Silicon Valley began when William Shockley, a scientist who had led the team that developed the transistor at Bell Labs in New Jersey, decided that he wanted to manufacture transistors out of silicon in his own lab near his hometown of Palo Alto.

Although Shockley's firm eventually failed, the scientific talent he had assembled went on to create the framework that anchored Silicon Valley's phenomenal success.

Q. How do the securities markets work?

A. In school, most students don't learn a lot to help them understand the securities markets, and a lot of misconceptions remain. Here's a little help.

How does a stock transaction happen?

A seller and a buyer agree upon a given price for a given number of shares. Sometimes one or both parties are investors. In other cases, one is a "market maker" who deals in that security and is always willing to buy or sell it. At any given time, a stock has a current bid price (what someone is offering) and ask price (what someone will take). The distance between those is called the "spread." The transaction will occur when someone accepts someone's bid or asks for the right number of shares. A low number of shares traded daily is called "low liquidity" and is something for the investor to consider before shopping.

Can daring U.S. citizens buy foreign stocks?

The answer is a qualified yes, depending on the foreign stock. Many foreign stocks trade on U.S. exchanges as ADRs (American Depositary Receipts); a share of the ADR represents all the privileges of X number of shares on the underlying stock's home exchange. In some cases, foreign stock trades cost extra commissions. Easy clue: For any five-letter ticker symbol ending in F or Y [examples: NIPNY (NEC Corporation), BAYZF (Bayer)], the potential buyer is crazy if he or she doesn't first investigate the way the stock is traded. Foreign stock dividends may be subject to foreign tax, so don't be impressed by gaudy double-digit yields until you see how much gets skimmed this way.

How does a mutual fund work?

A mutual fund is simply an accumulation of invested assets in which investors own shares. The idea is that a professional can pick stocks or buy bonds more knowledgeably and wisely than you can, so you send that person your money to invest according to guidelines (clearly laid out in a prospectus). The share price of a mutual fund is called the NAV (net asset value) and fluctuates daily. The person you hired gets paid from the fund, typically collecting 1 percent of the total each year. Traditional open-end mutual funds issue and redeem shares as people buy and sell. A closed-end mutual fund issues a fixed number of shares and may trade above or below the NAV, because trades are brokered between shareholders rather than directly through the fund. An exchange-traded fund, or ETF, falls somewhere between the above.

Can I buy actual bonds?

You can, but only if you're pretty well funded and focused. The average investor will have a much easier time buying fixed-income mutual funds (open-end or closed-end). Bonds aren't traded on an open exchange the way stocks are; dealers sell them from inventories, typically in big blocks. When looking at a bond index, keep in mind that unlike stocks, no one can buy the index to assure getting its result, because the bonds in the index aren't always available at any price.

Is it actually possible for a person to make real money with stock dividends?

Sure, if that person is a smart investor. Very large company stocks tend to pay about 1.5 percent per year; you could beat that handily with good old bank CDs. But some smaller companies (and partnerships, and companies organized on specific models designed to pay large dividends) reliably pay 5 to 9 percent per year, which isn't chump change. The important thing is buying the shares at good prices, because dividends aren't really percentages—they're dollar amounts per share per period (often quarterly). The annual dividend divided by the stock price equals the yield percentage. Thus, if you are investing for dividends, you want a very low price because you'll get more shares, which will mean a bigger dividend check for as long as you hold the stock.

Q. Which labor strike was the first nationwide strike?

A. The Pullman strike of 1894. During the financial panic of 1893, demand for the company's train cars plummeted. Pullman laid off workers and cut the wages of those who remained by 30 percent. To make matters worse, Pullman, who was also his workers' landlord, continued to deduct the same rent from workers' paychecks to ensure investors would continue to get the 6 percent return Pullman had promised them. In response, the American Railway Union (ARU), led by Eugene Debs, called for a strike. Railroad workers across the nation refused to handle Pullman cars. The strike became a national issue. President Cleveland declared the strike a federal crime and deployed 12,000 troops. The strike ended on August 3, 1894, and many workers and their supporters around the country were devastated as the Pullman employees were forced back to work. The Pullman strike left 13 strikers dead and 57 others wounded.

Q. Where is the premier wine-growing region in the United States?

A. The Napa Valley in California. Its viticultural history began in 1836 with George Calvert Yount, an early settler who planted the region's first vineyards. By 1860, other grape growers had arrived, and in 1861, Charles Krug established the first commercial vineyard. By the late 19th century more than 140 vineyards were operating in the region. The area had its ups and downs over the next several years, but it was revived in the mid-1960s when Robert Mondavi opened the first modern vineyard in the area. In 1999 Napa Valley was named one of nine "Great Wine Capitals" around the world.

Q. What American companies were broken up in 1911 as a result of antitrust proceedings?

A. American Tobacco and Standard Oil. American Tobacco, one of the original 12 members of the Dow Jones Industrial Average, attracted the attention of regulators after it acquired Lucky Strike and more than 200 rival companies. Antitrust proceedings started in 1907, and in 1911, the American Tobacco Company ceased to exist, having been broken up into several different companies. Standard Oil controlled 91 percent of American oil production in 1904. The Department of Justice sued Standard Oil in 1909 under the Sherman Antitrust Act. The U.S. Supreme Court ruled against Standard Oil, and the company was broken up in 1911.

Q. Who were the original members of the Dow Jones Industrial Average?

A. The original 12 members of the Dow Jones Industrial Average are as follows:

1. **American Cotton Oil** later became Bestfoods, which is now part of Unilever.

2. **American Sugar** became Domino Sugar in 1900 and is now called Domino Foods, Inc.

3. **American Tobacco** was broken up in 1911.

4. **Chicago Gas** was acquired by Peoples Gas, which is now part of Integrys Energy Group.

5. **Distilling & Cattle Feeding** is now Millennium Chemicals.

6. **General Electric** is the only one of the original 12 still operating under its original name.

7. **Laclede Gas** now operates as the Laclede Group, Inc., but has not been part of the Dow Jones Industrial Average since 1899.

8. **National Lead** is now NL Industries but has not been part of the Dow Jones Industrial Average since 1916.

9. **North American** was an electric utility holding company. The Securities and Exchange Commission (SEC) broke it up in 1946.

10. **Tennessee Coal, Iron and Railroad** was acquired by U.S. Steel in 1907.

11. **U.S. Leather** was dissolved in 1952.

12. **United States Rubber** became Uniroyal in 1961, merged with B.F. Goodrich in 1986, and was bought by Michelin in 1990.

Q. What was the first major credit card?

A. According to *The Flintstones*, credit cards have been around since the days when humans coexisted with dinosaurs. The cards were carved from stone, and shoppers headed out into the wild searching for bargains while uttering a guttural, "Charge it!"

In reality, the story goes back only as far as 1949. Frank McNamara, head of a credit corporation, and two friends had finished dining at a New York City restaurant, and Frank reached into his pocket to pay for the meal. All he found was lint—he had forgotten his wallet. To avoid washing dishes, McNamara opted for the slightly less embarrassing solution—calling his wife and asking her to bring money.

This brush with empty pockets gave Frank an idea. What if instead of stores each issuing their own lines of credit, thus requiring people to tote around dozens of cards, there was one card that could be used in various places? Since this would require a middleman between customers and businesses, Frank figured he might as well snag the position for himself. And, thus, the Diner's Club card was born.

In 1950, Diner's Club distributed 200 cards, mainly to McNamara's friends and associates, most of whom were salespeople. Since they had to entertain clients with meals, it was a perfect scenario—they could go to any of the participating restaurants and simply charge their food and drinks.

The first card was not made of plastic—it was paper, with a list of the participating restaurants on the back. Initially, only 14 restaurants were included, but the idea soon caught on. By the end of 1950, there were 20,000 card members and 1,000 participating restaurants.

After McNamara sold his share of the company in 1952, the Diner's Club concept continued to grow. The card went national and worldwide, eventually facing competition from American Express, Visa, MasterCard, and

others. In early 1981, Citibank bought Diner's Club. In April 2008, Discover Financial Services bought Diner's Club International from Citibank for $165 million. Not bad for a guy who couldn't afford to pay for dinner.

Q. Does it cost more to make a penny than a penny is worth?

A. When someone offers a penny for your thoughts, you may want to ask for more. In late 2007, the United States Mint reported that its cost to make a penny was 1.67 cents (7.4 billion were minted that year); in May 2008, the cost had dropped to 1.26 cents. At either rate, U.S. taxpayers were not getting their money's worth.

The production cost of a penny includes materials, labor, processing, and transportation. And these expenses don't adversely affect only the penny. Nickels also are worth less than their cost to produce. Making a five-cent piece runs nearly ten cents.

In 1792, the newly created U.S. Mint introduced the penny as an all-copper coin. Since 1857, it has been an alloy of copper and other metals, typically zinc. With copper prices on the rise, Congress voted in 1982 to change the coin's composition to 97.6 percent zinc core and 2.4 percent copper plating. This made economic sense in 2005, when it cost 0.97 cent to make a penny. But zinc and copper prices increased after that, sending penny production prices soaring beyond a penny.

Some believe that the penny has long outlived its usefulness and should be retired, but it is more likely that Congress would instead vote to change the penny's composition again. Metal prices fluctuate, and the cost of making coins rises and falls accordingly. (Congress has changed the penny's composition half a dozen times over the years.) So don't look for the penny to disappear anytime soon.

Q. Who was the first secretary of the U.S. Treasury?

A. Alexander Hamilton. Known as the great architect of America's financial system, Hamilton argued that the states should be subservient to a powerful federal government that could better formulate an economic policy for the benefit of all. He introduced controversial new taxes, paid off the country's war debts, and established a national bank.

Q. Which American business tycoon funded nearly 3,000 public libraries around the world?

A. Andrew Carnegie. Over the course of his rags-to-riches life, the steel giant donated $350 million to cultural and educational institutions, scientific research, and the cause of peace. He is best known as the benefactor of public libraries, funding nearly 3,000 of them around the world.

Q. Why does the price of many products end in 95 or 99?

A. It seems like it would be a lot simpler for both retailers and consumers if the price of that $29.95 toy was instead a nice, round $30. There must be a good reason why the prices of so many products end in 95 or 99. But what is it?

Two theories stand out. One suggests a ploy to coerce the customer into a purchase, the thought being that a price of $29.95 seems more palatable than one of $30 (though sales tax would

likely shove the total over $30, anyway). This theory seems plausible, even if it doesn't place much value on our intelligence.

The practice of ending prices in 95 or 99 began in the late 1880s, when newspapers started carrying store advertisements that included prices, says Scot Morris, a self-described collector of "strange facts and useless information." By advertising an item at 99 cents instead of a dollar, a store could undercut its competition and, theoretically, gain customers. This practice wouldn't cost the store much money, and customers would feel like they were saving money—everyone would be happy.

A second theory focuses on a big problem in the retail business—employee theft. According to this explanation, if an item's price is a round number, it's easier for an employee who's handling the cash register to pocket the money handed over by the customer. The customer is more likely to have the exact amount if the cost is an even $30, which means that the clerk doesn't have to open the register to provide change and can simply slip the money into a pocket. No record of the transaction exists, and the clerk can simply claim that the item was stolen if an issue arises. If a product costs $29.95, on the other hand, the employee probably will have to open the register to make change, and a record of the transaction will be created.

The loss-prevention theory might have once made sense, but it's less solid today considering the widespread use of credit and debit cards, not to mention sales tax. So we're left with the notion that consumers perceive a bigger difference between $29.99 and $30 than actually exists.

Robert Schindler, a marketing professor at Rutgers University, relates this to the impression that a price ending in 95 or 99 indicates a discount. He also cites the tendency of consumers to give diminished attention to rightmost digits in a price. Schindler compares this phenomenon to the hoopla surrounding certain birthdays, such as turning 40. It's just one year older than 39, but many of us feel the number 40 has much more impact. In this light, prices that end in 95 or 99 don't seem so strange after all.

Q. Is there a real Betty Crocker?

A. What began as a simple promotion—the chance to win a pincushion in the shape of a Gold Medal flour sack for correctly putting together a jigsaw puzzle— ended as a "woman" who towers over the culinary world. In 1921, the Washburn Crosby Company of Minneapolis (known today as General Mills) fielded so many questions related to the contest—and about baking in general—that it decided not to reply in an impersonal manner. Instead, the company created a homemaker-type character to answer the questions.

Thus Betty Crocker was born. Crocker came from William G. Crocker, a beloved retired director with the Washburn Crosby Company; Betty was a name that employees felt sounded wholesome and cheery. The now-famous Betty Crocker signature came from the hand of a company secretary, Florence Lindberg.

Betty Crocker quickly became a celebrity. In 1924, she hosted the first radio cooking show, *The Betty Crocker Cooking School of the Air*. Not bad for someone who didn't exist. The original radio voice for Betty Crocker came from Blanche Ingersoll, a home economist for the Washburn Crosby Company.

In the 1930s, Betty Crocker started advising Americans on how to prepare tasty meals within a limited budget. With the introduction of larger families, new appliances, and convenience foods in modern suburban homes, there was a growing need for recipes that were quick, easy, and inexpensive. Betty Crocker heard the call, and whisked her way to the rescue.

In 1936, Betty Crocker received a face to go along with her voice. Company artist Neysa McMein gathered all of the women in the Home Service Department together, and synthesized their profiles into a single matronly image. Betty Crocker was now well on her way to becoming an American icon. In fact, most of the country apparently thought she was real. According to a 1945 poll conducted by *Fortune* magazine, Betty was the second-most recognized woman in the United States, just behind Eleanor Roosevelt.

Betty Crocker has evolved eight times since those days. In 1980, for instance, her image morphed into that of a career-oriented go-getter, and in 1996, she acquired slightly darker skin and a more ethnic look.

A woman of countless talents, Betty Crocker has displayed a knack for writing. She's the author of more than two hundred cookbooks, including the wildly popular *Betty Crocker Picture Cookbook*, nicknamed "Big Red," which was first published in 1950 and is still in print today. For a time, it was second in sales only to the Bible.

Almost every pantry in America has at least one product festooned with a red spoon (the symbol of Betty Crocker), be it Hamburger Helper or Potato Buds. And most kitchens have a Betty Crocker cookbook. She is, quite simply, one of the most enduring figures who never lived.

Origins

Q. Who exactly is Uncle Sam?

A. Uncle Sam may be one of the most familiar icons to people in the United States, but no one is sure of the origins of this goateed, flag-theme-attired image. Was he an actual person or just snippets of people and images from popular culture?

During the War of 1812, the U.S. Army needed provisions and supplies—especially protein. Samuel Wilson, a meatpacker in Troy, New York, provided the troops with barrels of preserved meat, stamped "US," likely as a stipulation of his procurement contract. In fact, "Uncle Sam" was clean-shaven, short, and pudgy, the picture of a respectable merchant of his time, and he likely did not dress up for fun.

The Uncle Sam character we know today was born in the influential images of Thomas Nast, a prominent 19th-century political cartoonist who depicted several similar flag-themed figures.

The most enduring Uncle Sam image—which depicts him pointing a finger and saying "I Want You"—comes from World War I recruiting posters drawn by James Montgomery Flagg, who also modeled the famous stern, craggy visage.

Uncle Sam is actually a national personification—an image that sums up a national identity. Other countries' examples include John Bull of England—a stout, thick-necked, top-hatted guy—and Moder Svea (Mother Sweden), a sword-bearing woman in chain mail and a flowing skirt.

It wasn't until 1961 that Congress recognized Samuel Wilson as the original Uncle Sam. This didn't do Wilson much good, coming more than a century after his death, but it was a good deal for Troy, New York. The city began to pitch itself as the "Home of Uncle Sam," as it does today.

One popular beneficiary of the Uncle Sam concept was the band Grateful Dead, who used Sam's hat liberally in their imagery. Another is the New York Yankees, whose logo features Sam's top hat.

Q. Who started Mother's Day?

A. Celebrations of mothers date back to antiquity, but Mother's Day proper was the brainchild of Anna Jarvis. Raised in Grafton, West Virginia, Jarvis was the daughter of a woman who organized events called Mother's Friendship Days, which reunited West Virginia families that had been separated during the Civil War. After her mother died in 1905, Jarvis paid homage to her with an aggressive letter-writing campaign that began in 1907 and urged elected officials and newspaper editors to promote an official holiday to honor all mothers.

Within six years, most states observed Mother's Day. In 1914, President Woodrow Wilson signed a congressional resolution that designated the second Sunday in May as Mother's Day across the nation. Jarvis had succeeded, but little did she know that, just like Dr. Frankenstein, she had created a monster that would lead to her ruin.

Jarvis suggested that people wear white carnations, her mother's favorite flower, on Mother's Day. But when florists started charging more for carnations, she denounced the practice and chose instead to wear a button to commemorate the day. This was just one of many futile battles that Jarvis waged for the rest of her life against the quick and thorough commercialization of the holiday. Anybody who profited from Mother's Day felt her wrath. She considered Mother's Day cards especially nefarious, opining that giving one was a lazy way to show appreciation for the person who gave you the gift of life.

Jarvis lived off the considerable inheritances that she received after the deaths of her mother and her brother, Claude, who had founded a taxi service in Philadelphia. But while wholeheartedly devoting herself to fighting the exploitation of Mother's Day, Jarvis neglected to tend to her own finances. By 1943, she was living in poverty and her health was in serious decline. Friends raised enough money to allow her to live in a sanatorium in West Chester, Pennsylvania, where she died in 1948, childless.

If Jarvis were alive today, she wouldn't be at all pleased with what has happened to Mother's Day. In 2009, the National Retail Federation estimated total Mother's Day spending by consumers to be in the neighborhood of $14.1 billion.

Q. What's so American about apple pie?

A. Apple pie is so beloved in America that it's a cultural icon right up there with hot dogs, baseball, and Chevrolet. Funny thing is, the double-crust pastry that is filled with fruit and seasoned with cinnamon wasn't even invented in the United States.

Was that your dessert fork dropping to the floor? Think about it. Apples aren't indigenous to the United States—English colonists brought them here. Remember the story of Johnny Appleseed? Truth be told, apple pies were being baked long before settlers arrived on North American shores. In fact, pie has been around in one form or another since the ancient Egyptians first created the pastry crust. The Greeks and Romans, for example, made main-dish pies filled with meat.

According to the American Pie Council, the first fruit-filled pies or tarts (called "pasties") were likely created in the 1500s. In the Tudor and Stuart eras, English pies were made with cherries, pears, quinces, and—yes—apples.

So okay, apple pie isn't innately American. It came here with the first settlers. But gosh darn if we didn't perfect it and make it all our own. You see, the early English apple pies were usually made without sugar. And the crusts were often tough and inedible, used more for holding the filling together than for eating.

According to *The Oxford Encyclopedia of Food and Drink in America*, the typical American pie evolved to be made with uncooked apples, fat, sugar, and sweet spices. Now we're talking! No wonder the phrase "as American as apple pie" came to be.

Whether you like your apple pie baked in a paper bag, à la mode, or topped with a slice of cheddar cheese, we took someone else's recipe and turned it into a completely American experience. Heck, apple pie is even on the menu at McDonald's. That's about as American as it gets.

Q. ■ Why doesn't the United States use the metric system?

A. ■ For many Americans who have driven into Canada, the most immediately noticeable difference is the way things are measured. Distances are shown in kilometers and gas is sold by the liter, which can be confusing when you're used to miles and gallons. American travelers in Europe, or pretty much anywhere else in the world, face the same problem. Why does the United States stubbornly cling to its own idiosyncratic system of weights and measures, when the metric system is easier to use and universally recognized? Liberia and Myanmar are the world's only other countries that have not adopted the metric system.

Well, this turns out to be a bit of a trick question, because in many ways the United States *has* adopted the metric system. An 1866 law made it legal to use metric measurements in contracts and agreements. In 1893, the United States set the official definitions of U.S. units based on metric units. One U.S. pound equals 453.59237 grams, for example. And the Metric Conversion Act of 1975 (among several other laws passed over the decades) encouraged the adoption of metric units by American science and industry. For the most part, American scientists and businesses (especially those that sell goods to other countries) use the metric system every day.

What the United States hasn't done is ban the use of non-metric measuring systems. A country can pass all the laws it likes encouraging the use of a new system, but humans are naturally resistant to change. Americans like their familiar miles, pints, yards, and acres. Until it becomes illegal to use the old system, the average American will stick with it.

In fact, even an all-metric law is no guarantee. Britain (upon whose Imperial weights and measures system the United States based its own) has been struggling with the metric system for decades. Traditionally, the British have preferred their old Imperial classifications, but their proximity to the rest of Europe has forced generations to learn both systems. Laws requiring the abandonment of Imperial units by shops and businesses in recent years were ignored by a few "metric martyrs," and eventually the European Union gave up trying to force the metric system on unwilling Brits. So fear not, Americans—you're not in any imminent danger of losing your time-honored miles, gallons, and inches.

Q. What does the "D" stand for in D-day?

A. D-day—June 6, 1944, the day that Allied forces began their invasion of northwest Europe in World War II—was an extraordinary moment. In one of the largest and most dangerous assaults in military history, the Allies stormed the beaches of Normandy, France. It is generally regarded as the most significant operation in the war.

There are many possible dramatic d-words that describe the day: doom, deliverance, death. But *the* "D" comes from the word "day." D-day is a generic military term meaning, in the words of the U.S. Department of Defense *Dictionary of Military and Associated Terms*, "the unnamed day on which a particular operation commences or is to commence." The term came into use during World War I as a way of referring to the day of a military operation before a specific date was set. In planning an operation, the military uses D-day as a time reference. For example, D – 3 means three days before D-day; D + 1 means the day after D-day.

A related term is H-hour, the actual hour the operation will begin. In the case of an amphibious assault, that would be the time the first soldiers land. The exact time line for a D-day is described in reference to H-hour. At Omaha Beach (the code name for one of the main landing points of the Allied invasion at Normandy), the planned time line called for tanks and trucks to move inland at H + 120 minutes, or two hours after the assault on the beaches began.

The "D" in D-day is fairly mundane, hardly befitting of one of the most monumental days in American history.

Q. ■ Why do U.S. soldiers wear a backward American flag on their shoulders?

A. ■ It's a symbol of good old-fashioned bravery. The flag patches on the U.S. Army uniform are the modern-day observance of a time-honored tradition — carrying flags into battle. But instead of schlepping a big flag on a pole onto the field, as a standard bearer would have done in the Revolutionary War or Civil War, modern soldiers simply wear flags on their uniforms.

To keep true to the tradition, there's an imaginary pole leading the way. The army regulation states that the flag should "be worn so that to observers, it looks as if the flag is flying against a breeze." On the right shoulder, this means the stars—the "union," in flag-speak—are on the right. The same goes for flags on the right side of vehicles and aircraft. If the flag were pointed the other way, with the union on the left side, it would be as if the soldier was carrying the flag away from the battle. And that's not how the army rolls.

If you think about the patch that way, the flag isn't really backward. After all, you wouldn't say a flag on a pole was backward if you saw it from the side and the stars were on the right. But it rightly seems backward, because the flag code dictates that whenever the flag is against a wall, as in artwork, the union should be to the left.

At any rate, don't try this at home, unless you want the flag-code police banging on your door. Leave the "backward flags" to the professionals.

Q. Why is the U.S. presidential election held on a Tuesday in November?

A. Blame it on Congress. Before 1845, the U.S. presidential election was held during the first week of December. But that year, Congress designated November as the election month for both the president and members of Congress because November's weather is typically milder than December's. This, Congress felt, would ensure a better turnout since most Americans lived in rural areas back then and had to travel long distances by foot or on horseback to reach voting sites.

Why Tuesday? Some men (only white men could vote, remember) had to leave home a day in advance. A

Monday election meant leaving home on Sunday, the day of worship. Friday or the weekend were not considered good options either. As is the case today, weekends were booked with travel, shopping, and other business. And Thursday? That was Britain's election day, and the United States didn't want its political process to resemble Britain's in any way. Tuesday and Wednesday were the only other possibilities, and Tuesday was chosen.

Does it matter which Tuesday in November? Yes. It's always the Tuesday after the first Monday in November, which means elections will never be held on the first day of the month. Why is this important? When the decision was made, many small businesses were closing out their October books and balancing their ledgers on that day. Furthermore, November 1 is a Catholic holiday (All Saints' Day), which might have kept some men away from the voting booths.

The first election following the enactment of these rules took place on November 4, 1845. It wasn't a presidential contest—members of Congress were elected—but it nonetheless marked the beginning of an American tradition.

Q. How did Labor Day get started?

A. Next time you're enjoying time off for Labor Day, relishing cold beer and grilled bratwurst in the backyard, you can thank Peter J. McGuire of New York. Or maybe Matthew Maguire (no relation).

In the 1880s, Peter J. McGuire, one of the cofounders of the American Federation of Labor (AFL), is said to have developed the idea of a holiday for American workers in homage to those "from whom rude nature have delved and carved all the grandeur we behold." On the other hand, Matthew Maguire, a machinist and secretary of the Central Labor Union (CLU), is also credited with that honor.

In any case, the CLU and the Knights of Labor decided to go ahead with the holiday in New York City, and the first Labor Day was observed on September 5, 1882, with a grand parade and festival in Union Square. By 1885, as the labor movement continued to gain ground and organized labor lobbied vigorously in state legislatures, Labor Day was celebrated in cities around the country. The first Monday of September was agreed upon as the official date, roughly halfway between the Fourth of July and Thanksgiving.

Prompted by widespread labor unrest, and perhaps the fact that 1894 was an election year, President Grover Cleveland was eager to appease the labor movement. On June 28, 1894, Congress unanimously named the first Monday in September a legal holiday. That didn't stop labor unrest—the 1894 Pullman strike was still going strong—but it was a step forward.

Today, Labor Day is still marked with speeches and celebrations, though with fewer of the large parades of the past. But many still regard it, as AFL leader Samuel Gompers did in 1898, as "the day for which the toilers in past centuries looked forward, when their rights and their wrongs would be discussed . . .

that the workers of our day may not only lay down their tools of labor for a holiday, but upon which they may touch shoulders in marching phalanx and feel the stronger for it."

Q. How did "The Star-Spangled Banner" become the national anthem of the United States?

A. As is the case with so many of the songs we know and love, "The Star-Spangled Banner" emerged from a fateful pairing of two potent forces — amateur poetry and alcohol.

On September 13, 1814, during the War of 1812, the British navy began a twenty-five-hour bombardment of Fort McHenry, Maryland, in an attempt to attack the city of Baltimore. A lawyer named Francis Scott Key witnessed the battle and, upon seeing the American flag raised in victory early the next morning, was moved to write a poem about it.

Just as you sometimes wake up in the morning with Debby Boone's "You Light Up My Life" inexplicably running through your head, Key had a tune rattling around in his noggin as the sun rose on September 14. It was "To Anacreon in Heaven," a popular British drinking song, and Key used its meter to guide his writing. The result was a four-stanza poem titled "The Defence of Fort McHenry." Key published the work almost immediately, along with instructions to sing the words to the tune of the drinking ditty. The poem was distributed throughout Baltimore. In October 1814, when it was published in sheet-music form, the song bore the more poignant title of "The Star-Spangled Banner."

The song steadily gained popularity throughout the 19th century, and by the time of the Civil War, it was a staple at patriotic events and had been played at its first baseball game at Brooklyn's Union Grounds Ballpark on May 15, 1862. By the 1890s, the song was a required component of military ceremonies, and in the early years of the 20th century, the push began to make it the U.S. national anthem. After about 20 years and more than 40 attempts at various bills and resolutions, Congress made "The Star-Spangled Banner" the national anthem on March 3, 1931. Before then, the national anthem was "My Country 'Tis of Thee."

It is customary to sing only the first of the song's four stanzas, which is probably just as well. A study done in 2005 revealed that 61 percent of Americans don't know all the words to even the first stanza. Furthermore, the second and third stanzas contain lyrics that are somewhat hostile to the British, and they're now our friends. During the queen's next visit to the United States, it probably would be considered poor taste to sing that British "blood has wash'd out of their foul footstep's pollution."

Landmarks, Monuments, and Attractions

Q. It's been called "America's Front Yard," but by what name is it better known?

A. The National Mall. When architect Pierre L'Enfant laid out his plans for Washington, D.C., in 1790, he envisioned a large, spacious avenue running down the center of the city. But it wasn't until 1851 that architect Andrew Jackson Downing was commissioned to design a landscape plan for the Mall. His plans called for a series of naturalistic parks and gardens with the Washington Monument as its centerpiece. In 1900, a new planning committee headed by Daniel Burnham reimagined the Mall, less as a series of naturalistic parks and more as a geometric open space lined with monuments and federal buildings.

The National Mall is truly a national treasure. On the east side is the Capitol, with the National Gallery of Art to the north. Museums of the Smithsonian Institution dot the landscape, and the Washington Monument is almost right in the middle. Here are seven memorials that should be part of any walking tour:

1. World War II Memorial
2. Vietnam Veterans Memorial
3. Lincoln Memorial
4. Korean War Veterans Memorial
5. Martin Luther King Jr. Memorial
6. Franklin Delano Roosevelt Memorial
7. Thomas Jefferson Memorial

Q. What iconic landmark in northwestern Arizona was declared a national monument in 1908 and became a national park in 1919?

A. The Grand Canyon. Although known to Native Americans for thousands of years, the Spanish didn't stumble upon the vast gorge until 1540. Significant American exploration of Grand Canyon wasn't undertaken until the 1860s. The land that became Arizona was not highly populated earlier in the 19th century, and the canyon itself did not become well known until after the Civil War. John Wesley Powell led the first known expedition down the Colorado River into the canyon in 1869. Almost immediately, the government attempted to protect this natural wonder, but miners and ranchers thwarted the effort. It wasn't until 1908 that Teddy Roosevelt declared the canyon a national monument, and in 1919, the Grand Canyon became a national park.

Q. Who gave Old Faithful its name?

A. In 1870, Henry Washburn, Nathaniel P. Langford, and Lieutenant Gustavus C. Doane set off on an expedition to explore what is now known as Yellowstone National Park. The men guided a group of more than a dozen explorers to discover a few of Yellowstone's most recognizable landmarks, including Old Faithful and Mount Washburn, which the group named themselves.

Q. How do you get a star on Hollywood's Walk of Fame?

A. They say you'll know you've made it in Hollywood when they give you your very own star on the Hollywood Walk of Fame, which is located along Hollywood Boulevard. But just how do all those celebs go about getting their very own star? Well, read on.

Who can apply for a star?
Anyone who makes/made their living in one of five categories:
- Live theater/performance
- Motion pictures
- Radio
- Recording
- Television

What criteria must a star applicant meet?
For someone to be considered for a star, the applicant must meet certain criteria:
- Professional achievement
- Longevity of at least five years in the field of entertainment
- Contributions to the community
- An agreement to attend the dedication ceremony

Who decides who gets a star?
Each year, the Walk of Fame Committee, which is part of the Hollywood Chamber of Commerce, is responsible for choosing from the submitted applications to select a new group of entertainers to receive stars on the Hollywood Walk of Fame. Once the Committee has made its selections, they still must be approved by the Hollywood Chamber of Commerce's Board of Directors and the City of Los Angeles' Board of Public Works Department.

How many people are awarded a star each year?

The Committee annually nominates up to 20 people to receive a star. On average, the Committee receives 300 applications per year.

Do you have to be alive to get a star?

No. Every year, one star is awarded posthumously. However, friends and family must wait five years after the entertainer's death before submitting an application. The Committee has been criticized for its failure to honor many industry pioneers because they lack a presence among the public and there are no family members to pony up the fee.

How much does each star cost?

Each recipient must pay $25,000 to the Walk of Fame Trust upon receiving his or her star.

What are the stars made of?

The stars are made of coral terrazzo with brass accents. The recipient's name is engraved on his or her star, along with an emblem identifying the category for which he or she has been honored: motion pictures, television, radio, recording, or live theater.

Can people choose where their star goes?

No, the stars are placed in areas as they are awarded. Stars are also faced in alternating opposite directions so that people walking either way on the sidewalk can read them.

What if an applicant doesn't get picked?

Applicants are permitted to reapply as many times as they like.

Q. Where can you find a full-size replica of the Parthenon?

A. Nashville, Tennessee. Built for the Tennessee Centennial Exposition in 1897 as a reflection of the city's nickname "The Athens of the South," it was never intended to be permanent, but it became so popular at the exposition that it was not torn down. A few years later, the building's temporary nature became undeniable, so it was rebuilt in concrete to become a permanent Nashville fixture.

Q. How many sites does the U.S. National Park Service administer?

A. The U.S. National Park Service administers about 400 sites of historic, scientific, cultural, scenic, or other interest. These include national monuments, national parks, national battlefields, national rivers, and national cemeteries. Here are some interesting details about U.S. national parks.

- Delaware is the only state with no national park territory.

- Although Yellowstone was the first national park (designated on March 1, 1872), it wasn't the first area set aside as a park. That honor is shared by the National Capital Parks, the White House, and the National Mall, all designated on July 16, 1790.

- National park status doesn't last forever. A couple dozen sites have been turned over to the states or to other federal departments. For example, the Park Service transferred New Echota Marker

National Memorial (a Cherokee heritage memorial) to the state of Georgia in 1950.

- The highest point in a national park is the summit of Denali (Mt. McKinley) in Alaska. At 20,320 feet, it's also the highest point on the North American landmass.

- In Alaska's Kobuk Valley National Park, there are approximately 25 square miles of rolling sand dunes, and summer temperatures can hit 100 degrees Fahrenheit.

- The lowest point is Badwater Basin in California's Death Valley National Park, which is 282 feet below sea level. From 1931 to 1934, just over half an inch of rain fell there, and summer temperatures can exceed 130 degrees Fahrenheit.

- Death Valley National Park also has a mountain, Telescope Peak, which tops out at 11,049 feet above sea level. From the top of this mountain to Badwater Basin, it's twice the vertical drop of the Grand Canyon.

- The northernmost point in a national park is Inupiat Heritage Center at Barrow, Alaska; the southernmost point is the National Park of American Samoa, below the equator.

- The farthest national park from Washington, D.C., is War in the Pacific National Historical Park in Guam. It's far closer to the Philippines than to Hawaii, let alone the continental United States.

- The longest arch at Arches National Park in Utah measures 306 feet from base to base. A football field is 300 feet long.

- Oregon's Crater Lake National Park is a corpse—a volcanic corpse, that is. Ancient Mt. Mazama coughed up one last violent eruption in the earliest stages of human civilization, then its walls collapsed into the dead volcano's caldera. Precipitation fell and melted to form a shimmering six-mile-wide lake.

- Devil's Tower in Wyoming began its history buried—a tall pillar of magma that leaked or burned through the other rock in the area, then cooled underground. Millions of years of erosion laid bare the 1,267-foot tower.

Q. When did the iconic Empire State Building open to the public?

A. 1931. When the Empire State Building opened in 1931, it was the world's tallest structure, soaring 1,454 feet from the ground to the top of its lightning rod. More than 3,000 workers took less than 14 months to build the structure, with the framework erected at a pace of 4.5 stories per week. Designed by William Lamb, the Empire State Building is the crown jewel of the New York City skyline and is considered one of the strongest examples of art deco architecture. Today, visitors still marvel at the breathtaking views visible from the observatory, which on a clear day offers glimpses of the five surrounding states.

Q. When was the Golden Gate Bridge built?

A. Construction of San Francisco's Golden Gate Bridge began in 1933. The bridge, named for the Golden Gate Strait, which it spans, was the vision of chief engineer Joseph B. Strauss, who was told by contemporaries that such a bridge could not be built. Nevertheless, construction began on January 5, 1933.

Nearly four and a half years, $35 million, and 11 worker fatalities later, the bridge was finally opened to an estimated 200,000 pedestrians on May 27, 1937, and to vehicles the next day. Upon completion, it was the longest suspension bridge in the world.

The bridge is 1.7 miles long and 90 feet wide. It has two principal cables passing over the tops of the two main towers. If laid end to end, the total length of wire in both main cables would total 80,000 miles. The Golden Gate Bridge is painted "International Orange," making it more visible to ships and the 38 million vehicles that cross it annually in the lingering and persistent fog.

Q. What are some of America's famous monuments?

A. Here are a few of America's defining monuments:

Lincoln Memorial
"In this temple, as in the hearts of the people for whom he saved the Union, the memory of Abraham Lincoln is

enshrined forever." Beneath these words rests the Lincoln Memorial on the National Mall in Washington, D.C. Designed by architect Henry Bacon, sculptor Daniel Chester French, and artist Jules Guerin, the monument was completed in 1922 to honor the 16th president of the United States. The structure resembles a Greek Doric temple ringed by 36 columns, each representing a state in the Union at the time of Lincoln's death. Seated within the monument is a sculpture of Lincoln, and inscriptions from both the Gettysburg Address and his second inaugural address adorn the south and north walls, respectively. The Lincoln Memorial served as the site of Martin Luther King Jr.'s famous, "I Have a Dream" speech on August 28, 1963.

St. Louis Arch
The St. Louis Arch on the bank of the Mississippi River marks the city as the "Gateway to the West." Thomas Jefferson's vision of freedom and democracy spreading from "sea to shining sea" inspired architect Eero Saarinen's contemporary design for a 630-foot stainless steel memorial. Construction began in 1963 and was completed on October 28, 1965. The Arch's foundation is set 60 feet into the ground and is built to withstand earthquakes and high winds. A 40-passenger train takes sightseers from the lobby to the observation platform, where on a clear day the view stretches for 30 miles.

Washington Monument
The Washington Monument, a 555-foot-high white obelisk situated at the west end of the National Mall in Washington, D.C., honors George Washington as the first president of the United States and a Revolutionary War hero. Comprised of 36,491 marble, granite, and sandstone blocks, the structure was designed by Robert Mills, a prominent American architect. Construction began in 1848, but due to the outbreak of the Civil War and lack of funding, it took nearly 40 years to complete.

It is clearly visible where work resumed in 1876 by the difference in the marble's shading, about 150 feet up the obelisk. The monument was dedicated in 1885, on Washington's birthday, February 22, but did not officially open to the public until October 9, 1888, after the internal construction was complete. At the time, it was the world's tallest structure, a title it held only until 1889, when the Eiffel Tower was completed in Paris.

Statue of Liberty

The Statue of Liberty is perhaps the most enduring symbol of America and has become a universal symbol of

freedom and democracy. Located on a 12-acre island in New York Harbor, the Statue of Liberty was a friendly gesture from the people of France to the people of the United States. The statue, designed by French sculptor Frédéric Auguste Bartholdi, was dedicated on October 28, 1886, designated a national monument in 1924, and underwent a face-lift for its centennial in 1986. Lady Liberty stands 305 feet and 1 inch high, from the ground to the tip of her torch.

Vietnam Veterans Memorial

The Vietnam Veterans Memorial in Washington, D.C., honors the men and women who served in the Vietnam conflict, one of America's most divisive wars. The memorial, intended to heal the nation's emotional wounds, was designed to be neutral about the war itself. Three components comprise the memorial: the Wall of Names, the Three Servicemen Statue and Flagpole, and the Vietnam Women's Memorial. The Wall was built in

1982 and designed by 21-year-old Maya Lin, who submitted the winning sketch. Visitors descend a path along two walls of black granite with one wing pointing at the Washington Monument a mile away and the other at the Lincoln Memorial about 600 feet away. When viewed closely, the names of the more than 58,000 soldiers killed or missing in action dominate the structure.

Q. How did Hersheypark in Hershey, Pennsylvania get started?

A. It was built in 1907 for the private use of Hershey Chocolate employees. It featured landscaped gardens and lawns and an outdoor theater where vaudevillians performed. Over the next few years, Hershey added more theaters, tennis courts, bowling alleys, and even a scenic railroad, while opening the park to the public. In 1912, a specially commissioned carousel was built, one of the largest of its kind at the time. In 1916, a zoo opened, stocked with Hershey's personal menagerie. By World War II, Hersheypark was one of the prime tourist destinations in Pennsylvania. After Disneyland opened and changed the expectation of theme parks, Hersheypark was retooled in 1971.

Q. Where is the Edmund Pettus Bridge, and why is it significant?

A. Selma, Alabama. It was the site of three civil rights marches in March 1965. The first, on March 7, was to protest the murder of unarmed civil rights protestor Jimmie Lee Jackson by an Alabama state trooper during a peaceful demonstration the previous month. Marchers intended to walk to Montgomery, but they could barely get across the bridge. Instead, the peaceful, unarmed marchers were savagely attacked by state troopers with billy clubs and tear gas. The ABC TV network interrupted its national programming to televise live footage of the violence. The resulting national outcry over the brutal police actions led to two larger marches over the next two weeks, both of which were led by Dr. Martin Luther King Jr. The last march, on March 21, ultimately saw nearly 25,000 people march into Montgomery.

Q. Who cracked the Liberty Bell?

A. Aside from the Statue of Liberty, the Liberty Bell might be the most enduring symbol of America. It draws millions of tourists to its home in Philadelphia each year. Yet for all of its historical resonance, anybody who has been to Independence Hall will attest that it's not the most attractive bell in existence. In fact, it looks kind of cruddy, due mostly to the enormous

crack that runs down its side. Whom can we blame for the destruction of this national treasure? No one has come forth to take responsibility, though there is no shortage of theories regarding the crack's origin.

A quick survey of the Liberty Bell's rich history shows that it has been fraught with problems since it was struck. The original bell, which was constructed by British bell-founder Lester & Pack (which is still in business today as Whitechapel Bell Foundry), arrived in Philadelphia in

1752. Unfortunately, it cracked upon its very first tolling—an inauspicious beginning for a future national monument. (On its Liberty Bell Web page, Whitechapel Bell Foundry repeatedly assures readers that good bell metal is "fragile.") Disgruntled Philadelphians called upon two local foundry workers, John Pass and John Stow, to recast the bell, with firm instructions to make it less brittle. The artisans did as they were told, but the new bell was so thick and heavy that the sound of it tolling resembled that of an axe hitting a tree. Pass and Stow were told to try again, and finally, in June 1753, the bell that we see today was hung in the State House.

Of course, in those days, it wasn't known as the Liberty Bell. It got that nickname about 75 years later, when abolitionists adopted its inscription—PROCLAIM LIBERTY THROUGHOUT ALL THE LAND UNTO ALL THE INHABITANTS THEREOF—as a rallying cry for the anti-slavery movement. By that time, the bell was already an important part of the American mythos, having been rung in alarm to announce the onset of the Revolutionary War after the skirmishes at Lexington and Concord, and in celebration when independence was proclaimed in 1776.

Exactly when the crack happened is a matter of debate amongst historians, though experts have been able to narrow it down to between 1817 and 1846. There are, in fact, several possible dates that are offered by the National Park Service, which is charged with caring for the bell (though it obviously wasn't charged with this task soon enough). The bell may have been cracked:

- in 1824, when it tolled to celebrate French Revolutionary War hero Marquis de Lafayette's visit to Philadelphia.
- in 1828, while ringing to honor the passage of the Catholic Emancipation Act in England.

- in 1835, while ringing during the funeral procession of statesman and justice John Marshall.

All of these theories, however, are discounted by numerous contemporary documents—such as newspaper reports and town-hall meeting minutes—that discuss the bell without mentioning the crack. In fact, the first actual reference to the Liberty Bell being cracked occurred in 1846, when the Philadelphia newspaper *Public Ledger* noted that in order for the bell to be rung in honor of George Washington's birthday that year, a crack had to first be repaired. The newspaper states that the bell had cracked "long before," though in an article published several years later, "long before" is specified as having been during the autumn of 1845, a matter of a few months.

Unfortunately, the paper gives no explanation as to how the bell cracked or who did it. Nor does it explain something that, when confronted by the crack in the bell, many viewers ignore: Not only were the bell-makers fairly shoddy craftsmen, they were also terrible spellers. In the inscription, the name of the state in which the bell resides is spelled "Pensylvania."

Q. Who was the first nut-job to go over Niagara Falls in a barrel?

A. In 1886, Carlisle Graham became the first person to strap himself into a barrel at Niagara Falls. Since then, a head-scratching assortment of nut-jobs have followed suit.

Niagara Falls, one of the natural wonders of the world, draws millions of visitors each year. It evokes awe and romance—but most of all, it seems to evoke the desire to climb into a barrel and plunge more than 150 feet. Okay, it only evokes that emotion in insane people, of whom there appear to be many—over the past 125 years, more than a dozen people have sealed themselves in barrels and gone for the wildest ride possible.

Niagara Falls has always been attractive to aspiring daredevils. Long before barrels became in vogue, Niagara Falls was the domain of tightrope walkers. The most famous of these was The Great Blondin, who made multiple high-wire trips across the breach. Funambulists still talk about the stunt that he pulled at the Falls in 1859, when he carried a stove out to the middle of the gorge and cooked an omelet before continuing to the other side.

The odd marriage of barrels and Niagara Falls began in 1886, when British cooper Carlisle Graham strapped himself into one of his barrels and did a little whitewater rafting in the whirlpools at the base of the Falls. Thus began a minor barrel-rafting fad that lasted until 1901, when a 63-year-old schoolteacher named Annie Edson Taylor—perhaps the least likely daredevil ever—kicked it up a notch. Taylor outfitted a barrel with some pillows and a mattress, climbed in, and then—to the astonishment of onlookers—proceeded to float over the edge of the Falls. Perhaps the only thing more astonishing than a sexagenarian schoolteacher coming up with this dumb idea was that she survived.

Since then, daredevils have attempted to mimic Taylor's stunt by going over the Falls in barrels made of wood, steel, rubber, and plastic, as well as by other means of conveyance, such as kayaks. Of course, several died. One man, Charles Stephens, thought it wise to tie an anvil to his feet; when he hit the water, the anvil crashed the barrel, tearing him apart. Another, Robert Overacker, attempted the stunt using a JetSki and a parachute—the only problem was that he forgot to fasten the parachute to his back.

Then there's Bobby Leach, who became the first male to successfully go over the Falls in a barrel in 1911. A few years later, however, he met his maker. How? By slipping on an orange peel.

Q. Where are the most romantic kissing spots in America?

A. What makes a place romantic enough to inspire a long, passionate kiss? The answer differs for all couples, but one universal answer seems to apply: Being together in beauty—whether in a natural setting or a creation of the human imagination—can certainly help affections flow freely.

Verde Hot Springs, Arizona
Hot passions won't cool off at these secluded hot springs. Wintertime water temperatures reach 96 degrees Fahrenheit and soar higher in summer. Soak in pools fit for two, or in seclusion underneath cliff overhangs.

Mendocino Headlands State Park, California
If the town of Mendocino wasn't tantalizing enough for romance, there's the adjacent state park where kissing spots are as common as tidal pools. Explore gentle pathways leading along rugged coastline to secluded beaches, hidden grottoes, and sea arches. On foggy days, a cool mist caresses cheeks and lips, so snuggle up to stay warm.

Amelia Island, Florida

A sun-kissed beach certainly qualifies as a smooching spot, but if lovers want more drama, Amelia Island delivers. More than just sand and surf, the island increases the pucker-up potential with delights of the Deep South: gnarled oak trees dripping with Spanish moss, footbridges crisscrossing windswept dunes, and wide, unspoiled Atlantic beaches. Study the birds and the bees while kayaking through gentle tidal creeks where egrets and herons await.

Chicago's Navy Pier Ferris Wheel, Illinois

Take to the sky to smooch! Nighttime is prime time to whirl around, snuggled together on a swinging seat, and view Chicago's fabulous skyline from this 150-foot-tall Ferris wheel.

Cumberland Falls, Kentucky

Bring a flashlight, hold hands, and venture deep into the woods to cast your eyes upon a romantically rare and unforgettable moonbow. A moonbow is a lunar rainbow that occurs at night, and Cumberland Falls (dubbed the "Niagara of the South") serves up this optical phenomenon on clear, moon-bathed nights. There's no pot o' gold at the bow's end, but the romantic reward of a moonlit kiss should prove satisfying enough.

McDonald Observatory, Texas

Like everything else in Texas, the night sky is big . . . and up in these parts it's darker than cowboy coffee—choice conditions for stargazing and kissing. At this remote observatory, starry-eyed lovers intent on romance can look toward the heavens for some unexpected celestial surprises but also find earthly delights. Relish romantic moments far from civilization (the nearest major town is 160 miles away), and be sure to wish upon a lone star.

Barboursville Vineyards, Virginia

Raise a toast to the state motto—"Virginia is for Lovers"—at this vineyard and winery nestled in the foothills of the Blue Ridge Mountains. As if sipping wine at a lovely vineyard wasn't enough to captivate your romantic attention, there are also enchanting ruins to explore. The remains of an early 19th-century mansion designed by Thomas Jefferson are tucked away in the boxwoods.

Providence Athenaeum, Rhode Island

Amidst the library stacks, there's romance and history . . . but not just in the books. Edgar Allan Poe spent hours hidden away in this 1838-era building reading poems to his love, Sarah Whitman. Choose your favorite love poem and tuck back into the stacks together for some riveting recitation of passionate passages.

White Sands National Monument Moonlight Walk, New Mexico

Moonlight has never before exerted such an attraction for lovers. When the moon's out in full force, these gypsum sand formations—the largest in the world—glow. Stroll hand-in-hand under the brilliant New Mexico night sky and steal a kiss under the approving eye of the man in the moon.

Q. How old is the White House?

A. The White House is more than 200 years old. Built between 1792 and 1800, it followed the architectural plans of James Hoban, but it has been

expanded over the years. The president and the First Family live in the main part of the building, while the president's offices are in the West Wing, which is connected to the Executive Residence by a colonnade originally designed by Thomas Jefferson.

Q. South Dakota's Black Hills are home to what famous patriotic sculpture?

A. Mount Rushmore. Gutzon Borglum was America's most famous sculptor in the 1920s, when he was

commissioned to work on this monumental project. Begun in 1927, the work took 14 years and nearly 400 workers to complete. George Washington, Thomas Jefferson, and Abraham Lincoln were obvious subjects for the sculpture, but Teddy Roosevelt had held the office of president just 19 years earlier.

Q. What are some WPA projects still used today?

A. During the Great Depression, the U.S. government stepped in to assist the needy and get the economy started again. Perhaps the widest-ranging and most productive New Deal measure was the Works Progress Administration (WPA), which provided more than $10 billion in federal funds from 1935 through the early 1940s and employed millions of people in hundreds of thousands of jobs. Here are some notable projects still in use today.

Camp David, Maryland
In 1936, the WPA began work on a recreational area in western Maryland's Catoctin Mountains, completing Camp Hi-Catoctin by 1939. For three years, it was used as a family camp for federal employees until President Franklin Delano Roosevelt visited in April 1942 and selected it as the location for presidential retreats. In the early 1950s, President Eisenhower renamed the camp for his grandson. Camp David has hosted dozens of visiting foreign dignitaries for casual meetings with U.S. presidents, but it remains closed to the general public.

Dealey Plaza, Texas
This park in the heart of Dallas was completed in 1940. Named for an early publisher of the *Dallas Morning News*, the plaza lives in infamy as the location of President John F. Kennedy's assassination on November 22, 1963. There may be other "grassy knolls" in American parks, but none have gone down in history like the one in Dealey Plaza.

LaGuardia Airport, New York
The Big Apple's desire for a city airport was only a dream until September 1937, when the WPA joined with the city to build one. Soon after opening in 1939, it was named New York Municipal Airport-LaGuardia Field to honor mayor Fiorello LaGuardia. The name was shortened to LaGuardia Airport in 1947.

Outer Bridge Drive, Illinois

In the heart of the Windy City, this bridge, which crosses the Chicago River near Lake Michigan, was started in 1929, but the Great Depression prevented its completion until the WPA delivered funds in the mid-1930s. When completed in 1937, the bridge was 356 feet long and

100 feet wide, making it the world's longest and widest bascule bridge. Also known as the Lake Shore Drive Bridge, it still stands today, forming part of the scenic Chicago waterfront.

Presidents

Q. Which six Civil War soldiers went on to be president?

A. Six Civil War soldiers not only survived the bloody conflict but went on to become the leader of the country. Fought primarily by young people, wars exert great influence in shaping a person's character and sometimes even his or her life path. The Civil War was no exception, serving as a proving ground for no fewer than six U.S. presidents.

Ulysses S. Grant
Grant rose to prominence during the war and was elected president in 1868 based on his service. He ran as a Republican in the first presidential election to follow his victory at Appomattox.

Rutherford B. Hayes
Almost 40 when the war broke out, Hayes volunteered and nearly lost his left arm to a musket ball in 1861. Following a miraculous recovery, he saw action in the Shenandoah Valley and ended the war as a major general. In 1877, he became president.

James Garfield
Garfield served under General Don Carlos Buell in Kentucky and at the Battle of Shiloh. In early 1862, he personally led a charge that drove Confederate troops out of the eastern part of the state. He left the army after the Battle of Chickamauga to take a seat in Congress in 1863, and he was elected president in 1880. Shortly after he took office, however, he was assassinated.

Chester A. Arthur

Although Arthur served the Union cause, he was nowhere near the front lines. He served as quartermaster general for the state of New York and was thus responsible for obtaining and delivering supplies to New York soldiers. He was ultimately awarded the rank of brigadier general. Elected vice president in 1880, he became president upon James Garfield's death.

Benjamin Harrison

Harrison raised a unit of volunteers in the Indiana Infantry and served as their colonel, later receiving a brevet promotion to general. Harrison was elected president in 1888, interrupting Grover Cleveland's two nonconsecutive terms.

William McKinley

The bloodiest single day of the war occurred at Antietam in 1862. Serving as a wagon driver under heavy enemy fire was one Sergeant William McKinley from Ohio. In the heat of the battle, he coolly drove two mule teams into the field at considerable personal peril to disperse food rations to hungry troops. His bravery that day won him a promotion to second lieutenant by his commanding officer—Rutherford B. Hayes. He was elected president in 1896 and 1900.

Grover Cleveland

The one president during the postwar years who didn't serve in the military was Grover Cleveland. His widowed mother's sole support, Cleveland hired a substitute to serve in his place. Although perfectly legal, this didn't endear him to Grand Army of the Republic veterans who were quite politically influential during

Cleveland's burgeoning political career. Nevertheless, he won election in 1884 and 1892.

Q. Which ten of the first twelve U.S. presidents owned or had owned slaves?

A. Here are the ten presidents that owned slaves:

1. George Washington
2. Thomas Jefferson
3. James Madison
4. James Monroe
5. John Tyler
6. William Henry Harrison
7. Andrew Jackson
8. James K. Polk
9. Zachary Taylor
10. Martin Van Buren

George Washington, Thomas Jefferson, James Madison, James Monroe, and John Tyler each came from Virginia plantation aristocracy. William Henry Harrison did too, although he moved to the free-soil Northwest Territories

and changed his slaves' status to indentured servants. Andrew Jackson and James K. Polk became wealthy as Tennessee lawyers; Jackson was even a slave trader for a time. Zachary Taylor owned a Mississippi plantation. The one Northerner among these Southerners, Martin Van Buren of New York, owned one slave before the practice was outlawed in his state. Of the early presidents, only John Adams and his son John Quincy Adams never owned slaves.

Q. Can an immigrant become president?

A. No. "No Person except a natural born Citizen, or a Citizen of the United States, at the time of the Adoption of this Constitution, shall be eligible to the Office of President." That's out of Article II of the Constitution. Because no one is still alive from 1788 (the year the Constitution was ratified), most legal scholars interpret this to say that one must be born to U.S. citizenship to be eligible for the presidency.

Q. How about vice president?

A. The Twelfth Amendment says that no one ineligible to be president can be elected vice president. However, that amendment mainly governs the meeting of the Electoral College—an important distinction. If the president appoints you vice president, you aren't elected.

Q. Can a two-term president run for vice president?

A. There's debate about it. The Twelfth Amendment seems to rule it out. The Twenty-Second

Amendment says you can't be elected more than twice; it doesn't say you can't run, just that the Electoral College electors cannot elect you. However, if the elected vice president died or resigned, the president could presumably appoint a former two-term president as vice president. Some argue that this means the former two-term president isn't constitutionally ineligible at all, and thus could actually be elected vice president. The Supreme Court prays it will never have to rule on the subject.

Q. **What does it really mean when we "impeach" a president?**

A. This caused a lot of confusion when it almost happened to President Richard Nixon. Everyone assumed "impeach" meant "remove." It doesn't. If you impeach someone, you have damaged that person's honesty or credibility. When Congress passes articles of impeachment against a president—which more or less translates to "The president has wronged"—it can then choose to vote to remove him or her. Andrew Johnson and Bill Clinton are the only U.S. presidents who have actually been impeached.

Q. **Which president was awarded the Navy and Marine Corps Medal for "extremely heroic conduct" in the South Pacific during World War II?**

A. Long before his days in the White House, John F. Kennedy proved his mettle in the South Pacific. In August 1943, 26-year-old Lieutenant John F. Kennedy was serving as the skipper aboard PT-109, a high-speed boat assigned to patrol the Pacific and sabotage Japanese supply lines.

In the early morning of August 2, 1943, Kennedy's PT boat was split in two by the Japanese destroyer, *Amagiri*. As his crew floated in the shark-infested water, JFK led them in a search for safety and rescue in a famous six-day ordeal.

After the collision, the surviving crew of PT-109 assembled on the wreckage of the boat's bow to discuss their options. They decided to set off for Plum Pudding Island, a tiny dot of land deemed too small to interest the Japanese. The crew swam for hours, Kennedy towing an immobile Patrick McMahon through the water by clenching the strap of the badly burned man's life jacket in his teeth. They stumbled to shore across the razor-sharp coral, and Kennedy, having swallowed copious amounts of seawater, vomited and collapsed on the beach.

After he recovered, Kennedy announced that he intended to swim the mile and a half into the sea and attempt to contact PT boats on their patrol that evening. Ensign Barney Ross thought the plan was absurd; McMahon thought it was suicidal. Nevertheless, Kennedy was determined to try. At about 6:30 P.M., he slipped back into the water, walking as far as he could on the surrounding reef before swimming out into the deeper channel. Unbeknownst to the survivors, the American fleet had shifted its patrol area miles to the north, and no boats came that night. By 9:00 the next morning, the men on the island assumed the lieutenant must be dead, only to be proved wrong around noon when he dragged himself back ashore. Despite Kennedy's lack of success, he ordered a skeptical Ensign Ross to make a similar attempt that night. Unfortunately, Ross's effort proved no more effective.

The men exhausted the resources on Plum Pudding by the second day. Driven by a need for more food and the desire to be closer to potential rescuers, Kennedy decided to move the group to another island, Olasana, covered with plenty of coconut trees and located closer to the PT patrol area itself. Again, Kennedy towed McMahon, who by now had difficulty seeing due to scabs forming over his burned eyelids.

Naru and Encounters with the Japanese

The next day, Kennedy and Ross decided to swim to the neighboring island of Naru. Kennedy had no real hope for the effort, but he wanted to remain active to keep up his men's morale. Searching the island, Kennedy and Ross found the wreckage of a small Japanese boat containing a crate filled with crackers and candy, as well as a small dugout canoe with a supply of water. Discussing their windfall, the two men made their way back down to the beach.

As Kennedy and Ross emerged onto the beach, they immediately spotted two other men out on the reef. Convinced that they had encountered the Japanese, they quickly dived back into the bushes. The two strangers in question, Melanesian scouts, Biuku Gasa and Eroni Kumana, were actually in the employ of the Australian military. Convinced that Kennedy and Ross were themselves Japanese, the two natives leapt into their canoe and furiously paddled away, fortunately heading toward Olasana, where the remaining PT survivors were camped. Making contact with the crew, the islanders helpfully offered the information that Naru contained Japanese troops, much to the alarm of the PT crew. Little did they know that one of the "Japanese" Biuku and Eroni referred to was actually their own skipper.

Coconuts and Rescue

Returning to Olasana in the canoe the next day, Kennedy found Ensign Leonard Thom chatting away with Biuku and Eroni. The scouts were sent off with two messages, one written with the stub of a pencil Thom had somehow managed to keep throughout the entire ordeal; Kennedy carved the other into the side of a coconut. The coconut read, "NARU ISL / NATIVE KNOWS POSIT / HE CAN PILOT / 11 ALIVE / NEED SMALL BOAT / KENNEDY." The news quickly made its way back to Lieutenant Arthur Reginald Evans, an Australian coast-watcher near Wana Wana, who had actually seen the wreckage of PT-109 and sent messages to the Americans for several days inquiring about the possibility of survivors. Evans dispatched a larger canoe with supplies. Kennedy made his way back to Wana Wana in the larger canoe, hiding from Japanese air patrols under palm fronds in the bottom of the boat. He met Evans and rendezvoused with a PT-boat patrol bound to pick up his shipwrecked crew, who were rescued on August 8. Except for the two men lost in the initial collision, the crew of PT-109 survived.

Controversy erupted surrounding the loss of PT-109. General MacArthur thought Kennedy should face court-martial, but the official Navy report was much less critical. However, regardless of the circumstances of the loss, John F. Kennedy's determined efforts to save his crew were beyond question. Lieutenant Kennedy was awarded the Navy and Marine Corps Medal for "extremely heroic conduct." Kennedy himself, however, felt as if he hadn't accomplished enough in the war and turned down an offer to return home, instead making a successful effort to obtain command of another boat.

John F. Kennedy eventually rose to a much greater position than that of a junior officer in the South Pacific. He kept the famous coconut on the desk in the Oval Office throughout his presidency. Despite all of his other successes, in 1963 he wrote, "Any man who may be asked in this century what he did to make his life worthwhile, I think can respond with a good deal of pride and satisfaction, 'I served in the United States Navy.'"

Q. How many U.S. presidents have hailed from Ohio?

A. Seven United States presidents have hailed from Ohio.

Ulysses S. Grant
Rarely is a president better known for his military accomplishments than political feats, but Ulysses S. Grant, the 18th president of the United States, goes down in history for his role in the Civil War.

Benjamin Harrison
The only father-son presidential pairings are John Adams/ John Quincy Adams, and George H. W. Bush/George W. Bush. But Benjamin Harrison, born in North Bend, is the *grandson* of William Henry Harrison, 9th U.S. president and fellow Ohioan.

James A. Garfield
The 20th U.S. president, James A. Garfield, served in Congress for eight successful terms before being elected commander in chief. He died six months later after being shot by Charles J. Guiteau, a lawyer who was angry over being denied an ambassadorship.

Warren G. Harding
Warren G. Harding launched his career as a newspaperman in Ohio. His cabinet came to be known cynically as "The Ohio Gang," and his hard-line economic policies are

commonly blamed for the eventual outbreak of the Great Depression.

William McKinley

William McKinley declared war on Spain in 1898 after the *Maine*, a battleship that he had sent to Spanish-occupied Cuba, exploded. At war's end three months later, the United States acquired Guam, Puerto Rico, and the Philippines from Spain.

Rutherford B. Hayes

The election results between Rutherford B. Hayes and opponent Samuel J. Tilden, who won the popular vote, were heatedly contested.

William H. Taft

The 27th president of the United States, William H. Taft was born in Cincinnati, Ohio.

Q. What are some presidential nicknames?

A. Nicknames can be a measure of a president's notoriety or place in history. Few people remember the nicknames of lesser-known presidents such as James Buchanan ("Old Fogey") or Millard Fillmore ("The Wool-Carder President"). Yet other presidential nicknames have endured throughout history.

Theodore Roosevelt, deemed a great president by many, had quite a few memorable nicknames. Teddy Roosevelt was known as "The Trustbuster," who broke up giant corporations, and "The Rough Rider," whose wartime heroics in Cuba made him "The Hero of San Juan Hill." Yet Roosevelt was also cruelly dubbed "Old Four Eyes" for his pronounced myopia and "The Meddler" for his intervention in many sectors of society.

Abraham Lincoln was best known as "Honest Abe," but the 16th president had other monikers as well. His supporters hailed Father Abraham as "The Rail Splitter" and "The Great Emancipator." His detractors, playing on his long limbs, tagged him "The Illinois Ape." Abolitionists, who viewed him as weak on civil rights, called him "The Slave Hound from Illinois."

Presidents Bill Clinton and Ronald Reagan had an array of nicknames both good and bad. Clinton has been called "The Comeback Kid," "Bubba," and "Slick Willie." Reagan was dubbed "The Great Communicator," "The Gipper," and "Bonzo"—the latter a reference to the chimp costar of one of the ex-actor's films. Reagan also had a nickname any politician would crave: "The Teflon President"—meaning that few criticisms stuck to him.

It seems odd that the longest-serving president, Franklin Delano Roosevelt, had no lasting nicknames except for his initials, FDR. Shortening Roosevelt's name to initials set a precedent for some future chief executives, namely JFK (John Fitzgerald Kennedy), and LBJ (Lyndon Baines Johnson).

Some nicknames fit the character like a well-measured shoe. Feisty Harry Truman was dubbed "Give 'Em Hell Harry" after voters' shouts of support during his 1948 whistle-stop campaign. And a presidential nickname may never have fit better than the one for tight-lipped Calvin Coolidge: "Silent Cal." At one state dinner, a guest told Coolidge she had wagered friends that she could get at least three words out of the Sphinx of the Potomac. Coolidge replied: "You lose."

Many nicknames were hard to live down. The guileful

Richard Nixon was known as "Tricky Dick" and "The Trickster." And Chester A. Arthur was called "Prince Arthur" due to his weakness for fine clothes and accommodations. Grover Cleveland, who holds the record for most presidential vetoes, was dubbed "His Obstinacy." Worse, Cleveland was called "The Hangman of Buffalo" (while sheriff in Buffalo, New York, Cleveland personally slipped the noose around two felons). And the grandly named Rutherford B. Hayes was tagged "RutherFraud" after his disputed 1876 election.

Nicknames can be used for political advantage. Dwight Eisenhower used his for a catchy campaign slogan: "I Like Ike." (His college football moniker, "The Kansas Cyclone," was left on the sidelines.) George W. Bush used his mildly derisive nickname, "Dubya," to tweak opponent Al Gore's supposed invention of the Internet, noting that he himself was referred to as "Dubya, Dubya, Dubya," as in the World Wide Web.

One presidential nickname might have led to the most widely uttered phrase in English. Martin Van Buren, who hailed from Kinderhook, New York, was called "Old Kinderhook," which was then shortened to "OK." The name caught on.

Many recent nicknames, reflecting our less formal times, are simply shortened first names. Two notable examples are Bill Clinton and Jimmy Carter. Gerald Ford was often called Jerry. The more formal Ronald Reagan was only referred to as Ronnie by his wife, Nancy. And the name must suit the man: When Richard Nixon referred to himself as Dick it came across as forced informality.

Some nicknames are stirring, especially those gained in the military. Zachary Taylor was called "Old Rough and Ready" for his Spartan style of fighting the Mexican army. Andrew Jackson was named "Old Hickory" for leading a campaign against the Creek Indians while recovering from a dueling wound. William Henry Harrison was dubbed "Tippecanoe" to commemorate the name of his victorious battle in another Indian war. Ulysses S. Grant was known as "Unconditional Surrender" for his relentless leadership in the Civil War.

Yet some nicknames are deflating. As president of an often-ineffective government, Ulysses S. Grant was derided as "Useless" Grant. John Tyler was called "His Accidency" when he took office after the untimely death of William Henry Harrison. Franklin Pierce was dubbed "The Fainting General" for having been knocked unconscious during a Mexican-American War battle when his saddle horn collided hard with his stomach. James Madison, best known as "The Father of the Constitution," was vilified as "The Fugitive President" for fleeing Washington, D.C., during the British invasion of 1814.

And when then-Vice President John Adams suggested that George Washington be referred to as "His Majesty," Adams's foes were so irked by the regal, undemocratic-sounding title that they responded by sticking the stout VP with his own honorific: "His Rotundity."

Q. What does Harry Truman's middle initial, S, stand for?

A. Nothing. Harry Truman's parents, Martha Ellen and John, were unable to decide on a middle name for their firstborn son. Instead, they settled on the letter S, which could represent either his paternal grandfather (Anderson Shipp Truman) or maternal grandfather (Solomon Young).

Q. Who plotted to assassinate President Truman?

A. Puerto Ricans have sought independence from the United States for decades. In 1950, two ardent nationalists took matters into their own hands as part of a campaign to win independence through violent means. Their target? President Harry Truman.

Members of the Puerto Rican Nationalist Party were spoiling for a fight. They had tried—and failed—to reach their goal of independence through electoral participation. By the 1930s, party leader Dr. Pedro Albuzu Campos was advocating a campaign of violent revolution. Throughout the 1930s and 1940s, the Nationalist Party was involved in one confrontation after another. In 1936, Albuzu was charged with conspiring to overthrow the government and was incarcerated. He spent the next six years in jail in New York. When he finally returned to Puerto Rico in 1947, the tinder of nacionalismo puertorriqueño was bone-dry and smoldering.

The Match Is Lit
On October 30, 1950, Nationalists seized the town of Jayuya. With air support, the Puerto Rico National Guard crushed the rebellion. Griselio Torresola and Oscar Collazo, two nacionalistas, decided to retaliate at the highest level—the president of the United States.

They had help from natural wastage. The White House, which looks majestic from the outside, has been quite the wretched dump at many points in its history. By 1948, it was physically unsound, so the Truman family moved to Blair House. It would be a lot easier to whack a president there than it would have been at the White House.

The Attempt

At 2:20 P.M. on November 1, 1950, Torresola approached the Pennsylvania Avenue entrance from the west with a 9mm Luger pistol. Collazo came from the east carrying the Luger's cheaper successor, the Walther P38. White House police guarded the entrance. Truman was upstairs taking a nap.

Collazo approached the Blair House steps, facing the turned back of Officer Donald Birdzell, and fired, shattering Birdzell's knee. Nearby Officers Floyd Boring and Joseph Davidson fired at Collazo through a wrought-iron fence but without immediate effect. Birdzell dragged himself after Collazo, firing his pistol. Then bullets from Boring and Davidson grazed Collazo in the scalp and chest—seemingly minor wounds. Out of ammo, Collazo sat down to reload his weapon.

Officer Leslie Coffelt staffed a guard booth at the west corner as Torresola took him unaware. Coffelt fell with a chest full of holes. Next, Torresola fired on Officer Joseph Downs, who had just stopped to chat with Coffelt. Downs took bullets to the hip, then the back and neck. He staggered to the basement door and locked it, hoping to deny the assassins entry. Torresola advanced on Birdzell from behind as the officer engaged Collazo and fired, hitting his other knee. Birdzell lost consciousness as Torresola reloaded.

Weapon recharged, Oscar Collazo stood, and then collapsed from his wounds. At that moment, a startled Truman came to the window to see what was the matter. Torresola was 31 feet away. If he had looked up at precisely the right moment, the Puerto Rican nationalist would have achieved his mission.

Officer Coffelt had one final police duty in life. Despite three chest wounds, he forced himself to his feet, took careful aim, and fired. A bullet splattered the brain matter of Griselio Torresola all over the street. Coffelt staggered back to the guard shack and crumpled.

Collazo survived and was sentenced to death. Before leaving office, President Truman commuted Collazo's sentence to life imprisonment.

Officers Downs and Birdzell recovered. Officer Leslie Coffelt died four hours later. The Secret Service's day room at Blair House is now named the Leslie W. Coffelt Memorial Room.

Q. Who is the only U.S. president to become chief justice of the U.S. Supreme Court?

A. Most presidents have held other government positions before and after their time in office. But William Howard Taft is the only U.S. president to become chief justice of the U.S. Supreme Court. Taft, who served as president from 1909 until 1913, was appointed chief justice in 1921 by Warren G. Harding and served on the Court for nearly nine years.

Q. How many wives of U.S. presidents were crazy?

A. Good question. It's not easy to define crazy, and it is especially hard to judge the sanity of women who lived up to 230 years ago and kept their private lives private. Some presidential spouses, like Letitia Tyler (wife of John) or Margaret Smith Taylor (wife of Zachary), were recluses, either due to illness or temperament—but that doesn't make them crazy.

Jane Appleton Pierce may qualify. She and Franklin Pierce (who was an alcoholic) lost their young son in a train crash two months before Franklin was inaugurated as the 14th U.S. president in 1853. Jane fell apart; she'd already buried two children. She could not appear in public, and when Franklin Pierce left office, she had to be carried out of the White House. Her condition went beyond grief. She spent her time in Washington drowning in depression, or melancholia, as it was called then.

Abraham Lincoln was the 16th U.S. president—and if you haven't yet heard about the emotional ups and downs of his wife, pull up a chair. Mary Todd Lincoln was called unstable, hysterical, mad, and crazy throughout her life. She went on wild spending sprees that were kept secret from her husband. She threw raging fits about trifles and imagined threats. After her son died in the White House, Mary's crying binges and depression alternated with her manic extravagance and tantrums.

In her defense, Mary Lincoln suffered terribly from migraines, and she dealt with more tragedy during her lifetime than most people. After her husband's assassination, fear and pain drove her over the edge. Her hallucinations, paranoia, and screaming fits became too much for her adult son, Robert. He had Mary declared insane and committed to an institution for several months.

But was Mary Lincoln truly crazy? And if so, what mental illness did she have? Historians today are as divided in their verdicts as doctors and critics were back in the 19th century. The one thing they do agree on—grudgingly—is that the melancholic Abraham Lincoln was probably not the easiest man to live with. Maybe that's what made Mary crazy!

One other first lady, Ida McKinley, was also emotionally shattered by poor health (in her case, complicated by epileptic seizures) and the early deaths of her children. Her husband, William McKinley, cared for her tenderly, even after being elected president in 1897. She could do little in return except fold his black satin bow ties. Mostly, she crocheted bedroom slippers all day long. Ida lived until 1907, six years after her husband's assassination, but her illnesses were kept secret for years.

Q. **Which U.S. president served the shortest term?**

A. William Henry Harrison. Though some believed he died of a cold he caught during his inauguration on March 4, 1841, his death was due to pneumonia, which is caused by a virus, not cold weather. He died on April 4, after just 31 days in office.

Q. **Which president was known for his "fireside chats"?**

A. Franklin D. Roosevelt. Roosevelt often gave speeches on the radio, which came to be called "fireside chats." In these informal talks, it seemed as if the president were speaking directly to each American. Roosevelt explained to people what he was trying to do and often outlined what they could do to help. The president's smooth voice reassured worried Americans during the Great Depression and later, World War II.

Q. Which four U.S. presidents have been assassinated while in office?

A. Abraham Lincoln, James Garfield, William McKinley, and John F. Kennedy were assassinated while in office. James Garfield lived the longest before succumbing to his injuries. Abraham Lincoln was shot in the evening and passed away the following morning. William McKinley died of gangrene infection eight days after being shot. John F. Kennedy was pronounced dead half an hour after being struck by gunshots. But Garfield lingered for more than 11 weeks before dying of his gunshot wounds.

William McKinley

Abraham Lincoln

James Garfield

John F. Kennedy

Q. What's the difference between a commonwealth and a state?

A. Kentucky, Massachusetts, Pennsylvania, and Virginia style themselves commonwealths rather than states. In practice, there is no legal difference—a commonwealth enjoys no rights that a state does not, nor vice versa. During the Revolutionary period, it implied that the entity came together by mutual consent, but that applied to numerous states that call themselves states. There really is no difference whatsoever.

Q. Why is Louisiana law based on the Code Napoleon?

A. Because the United States bought Louisiana from the famed emperor. Louisiana judges rely less on precedent and more on their own interpretation of law than judges in other states. Louisiana law students decide whether to focus on American law or the Louisiana civil code. This situation, unique in U.S. jurisprudence, definitely keeps carpetbagging out-of-state lawyers from setting up shop in the bayou—unless they can be admitted to the Louisiana bar.

Q. Why doesn't Nebraska have a state senate?

A. The unicameral (having a single legislative chamber) Nebraska Legislature is actually more Senate than House of Representatives, but the state indeed has only one house. In the 1930s, Nebraskans felt that two legislatures wasted time and money, so they amended their state constitution to abolish the house and hand its duties to the Senate, now called simply the Nebraska Legislature. It also cut down the number of politicians. The Nebraska Legislature has 49 members, far fewer than other state legislatures.

Q. Which was the second state to give women the vote?

A. Utah—but the movement, coming from out of state, was hardly motivated by altruistic concern for women's political rights. Its supporters believed that Utah's women would dispense with polygamy if given the vote. The plan backfired on two levels. Not only did senior male Mormon leaders support it, but the majority of Mormon women voters continued to vote for polygamy. The gambit having bombed, the U.S. Congress canceled the women's suffrage in 1887. They got it back in 1895. Wyoming was the first state to give women the vote.

Q. What was Oklahoma's land lottery?

A. They trekked in by the tens of thousands to Oklahoma, by horse and by foot, under the blazing July sun. Hungry for land, they formed great lines, with hundreds sleeping in place. During this great 1901 migration, thousands of people camped out in one valley alone.

This was not the pell-mell, anything-goes 1889 land rush that gave Oklahoma Territory land to the "Sooners." No, this was quite the reverse. So contentious and confused had been the five land races between 1889 and 1895 that, to divvy up Oklahoma's remaining land, the federal government had opted for a civilized approach—a lottery. Vast crowds came from across the nation to register for the lottery.

Some groups were opposed to the giveaway. Ranchers wanted to continue grazing their stock on the lottery lands. Kiowa Chief Lone Wolf sued the Interior Department to keep the Indian lands settler-free.

Oklahoma Before the Lottery
From the end of the Civil War, the Indian Territory, later known as Oklahoma, had come under irresistible pressure for land. In 1866, the federal government coaxed the local Indian tribes into ceding two million acres. Soon, Anglo leaders such as William Couch were leading expeditions of "Boomers" (prospective settlers) into these "Unassigned Lands." In 1889, a group of Creek Indians—in defiance of the opposition of the "Five Civilized Tribes"—sold the government three million more acres. That same year, the Indian Appropriations Act opened 160-acre blocks of Oklahoma land to homesteaders on a first-come basis.

A multitude—50,000 on the first day—swarmed into Kickapoo country on horse, foot, and wagon. Many of the arrivals were former slaves. Thousands more—the Sooners—sneaked into the territories before the official start date. Gunfights broke out between Boomers and Sooners. Lawsuits between claimants dragged on for decades. Of every 14 Boomers, only one wound up with an irrefutable land claim. Four other land rushes through 1895 had similar woes. When the time came to redistribute the remainder of Oklahoma's turf, Washington resolved to find a better way.

A Better Way?
On July 4, 1901, President McKinley proclaimed that 4,639 square miles of land from the Comanche, Apache, Wichita, and Kiowa reservations would be parceled out on the basis of a vast lottery.

Registration for a chance to own a block of land took place at Fort Sill and in the town of El Reno, between July 10 and 26. Tens of thousands of would-be settlers swarmed in from Texas, Kansas, and, most of all, from settled parts of Oklahoma.

Under the arrangement, 480,000 acres of pasture were reserved for the Indian tribes, though most of this was leased to ranchers for pennies an acre. Thousands of Indians did receive homesteads; many Native Americans leased most of their acreage to farmers for a yearly per-acre fee of $1.50. Off-limits to the land rush were the War Department's Fort Sill and the Wichita Mountain Forest Reserve.

At the registration offices, each applicant filled out a card with his or her name, birthdate, height, and other identifying information. The cards were placed in large, wheellike containers for mixing and selection. Land parcels were divided into two huge swaths of territory around Lawton and El Reno.

As vast crowds waited to apply in heat over 100 degrees, trouble broke out. A Mexican was taken out and killed for trying to jump to the front of a registration line. People were required to notarize their applications. A mob almost lynched a fake notary, and lawmen arrested another notary who used an outdated seal. In the meantime, grifters and gamblers taking advantage of the bored multitudes waiting in line were banished from the streets. More welcome were painted Cheyenne Indians who offered spectators war dances for 25 cents.

Most registrants were farmers of limited income. No one owning more than 160 acres in another state was permitted to register. One registration card per person was the rule; hundreds trying to game the lottery with multiple applications were barred.

Single-day registration peaked at 16,700. In all, approximately 160,000 hopefuls signed up for a chance at 13,000 homesteads.

The Winners Are Revealed
Drawings began on July 29 in El Reno in front of 50,000 witnesses, whose tents and booths packed the dusty streets. From a platform on the grounds of a school, officials pulled the lucky registrations out of twin containers, representing the El Reno and Lawton parcels.

At 1:30 P.M., to a great hurrah, Commissioner Colonel Dyer called out the first name from the El Reno bin— Stephen A. Holcomb of Pauls Valley in Indian Territory.

The first lottery winner for Lawton was James R. Wood, a hardware clerk. The second was Miss Mattie Beal, a telephone operator from Wichita. After Commissioner Dyer read out her description—5-foot-3, 23 years old—the crowd cried: "They must get married!"

On August 6, winners began filing claims for their new properties at a land district office. There they got to choose the shape of their new 160 acres—a narrow strip, a square, or even the shape of a Z. In an unlucky stroke, 1,362 winners who failed to show up for the filings forfeited their claims for good.

The land rush immediately led to the creation of new Oklahoma counties—Comanche, Caddo, and Kiowa. Lots in the county seats were sold to raise some $664,000 to build roads, bridges, and a courthouse.

In 1907, boosted by the growing number of settlers and the economic growth that followed, Oklahoma became the 46th state.

Q. Can Texas really split into five states if it wants to?

A. Not really. This idea comes from a provision in an 1845 compromise governing the admission of Texas to the Union, motivated by the slave state-free state debate of that day. In 1861, Texas seceded and became a Confederate state. When it was readmitted in 1870, there was no such proviso, so don't expect the Lone Star State to become the Five Star States.

Q. What are the state nicknames for New England?

A. It may be part of the American character to give something a nickname. All the states have them. Some of these nicknames are official, having been voted on by the state legislature. In other cases, when nicknames haven't been a priority for state governments, the nicknames are simply informal.

- The official nickname of Connecticut is "The Constitution State," although it is commonly known as "The Nutmeg State," as well.

- Maine's state nickname? "The Pine Tree State."

- "The Bay State" is another name for Massachusetts.

- New Hampshire once had a strong quarrying industry, which provided its nickname, "The Granite State."

- Rhode Island is "The Ocean State." Although it's the smallest state in the Union, it is home to more than 400 miles of coastline. With Narragansett Bay cutting about halfway into its territory, you can never be more than 30 minutes away from salt water in Rhode Island.

- Vermont is known as "The Green Mountain State," which only makes sense. *Vert mont* is French for "green mountain."

Q. Which state is the birthplace of the highest number of U.S. presidents?

A. Virginia has been the motherland of eight future executives-in-chief: George Washington, Thomas Jefferson, James Madison, James Monroe, William Henry Harrison, John Tyler, Zachary Taylor, and Woodrow Wilson.

Q. What are the state nicknames for the Mid-Atlantic states?

A.

- Delaware calls itself "The First State," commemorating the fact that, on December 7, 1787, its legislature ratified the U.S. Constitution before any other state.

- Maryland's nickname goes back to the Revolutionary War. "The Old Line State" refers to Maryland's regiments fighting in the Battle of Long Island.

- New Jersey is "The Garden State," though no one can quite explain how it got that name.

- In 1785, George Washington referred to New York as "the Seat of Empire." From there, it's an easy jump to "The Empire State."

- For reasons not entirely clear, Pennsylvania is called "The Keystone State." This name likely goes back to the 1700s.

Q. What was notable about executive orders 10823 and 10860 of 1959?

A. These executive orders added stars to the flag in honor of Alaska and Hawaii, which both achieved statehood in 1959.

Q. What state holds the nation's gold reserve?

A. Kentucky. In 1936, construction began on the U.S. Bullion Reserve, using land adjacent to the Fort Knox army base in Fort Knox, Kentucky. Workers used over 1,400 tons of steel and 16,000 cubic feet of granite. The massive, more than 20-ton bombproof door to its vault is locked with a multifactor authentication lock that requires ten different Fort Knox employees to input a fraction of a larger combination; each employee's fraction is known only to that employee.

Q. What are the nicknames for the Midwest states?

A.

- The nickname of Illinois is "The Prairie State," although "Land of Lincoln" has been a popular name on state license plates.

- Indiana is known as "The Hoosier State." But what's a Hoosier?

- Iowa's nickname is "The Hawkeye State."

- Kansas is "The Sunflower State." It may come as no surprise, then, that the Kansas state flower is the sunflower.

- Michigan is called "The Wolverine State," although "The Great Lakes State" is also popular.

- Minnesota is "The North Star State," after the state motto, *L'Etoile du Nord*, which means "The Star of the North."

- The most popular nickname for Missouri is "The Show Me State." Although that is not an official nickname, according to Missouri's Office of the Secretary of State, it indicates "the stalwart, conservative, noncredulous character of Missourians."

- What will you find a lot of in Nebraska? Corn. Filled with people who can husk all that corn, Nebraska is called "The Cornhusker State."

- A number of nicknames are claimed by North Dakota: "The Peace Garden State," referring to the International Peace Garden shared by North Dakota and the Canadian province of Manitoba; "The Flickertail State," after the state's plentiful ground squirrels; and "The Roughrider State," in honor of Teddy Roosevelt's Roughrider cavalry from the Spanish-American War.

- Ohio is famously "The Buckeye State"—it has an awful lot of buckeye trees, which are the official state tree.

- The nickname of South Dakota is "The Mount Rushmore State," for obvious reasons. That nickname replaced "The Sunshine State," a name that had originally been featured on the state flag.

- Wisconsin's nickname, "The Badger State," remains unofficial, but the badger is the state's official animal, and it also serves as the mascot of the University of Wisconsin.

Q. Which is the only U.S. state that has had the flags of six nations flying over it?

A. Texas. The nations that have controlled it over the years are Spain, France, Mexico, the Republic of Texas, the United States, and the Confederate States of America.

Q. What state capital is also known as "Music City, USA"?

A. Nashville, Tennessee. Home of the Grand Ole Opry, Nashville is the traditional base for the country music industry. In the late 1800s and early 1900s a new style of music, which featured banjos, fiddles, and guitars, began to gain popularity in the American South. It had developed among the hill people of the Appalachians and other rural areas. Though this genre was originally known derogatorily as *hillbilly music*, it soon evolved into its own distinct genre, termed *country*.

Q. Why are the southern U.S. states called Dixie?

A.

I wish I was in the land of cotton,
Old times there are not forgotten,
Look away, look away,
Look away, Dixieland.

Where exactly is Dixieland? If you look on a map of the United States, you won't find it. Not a single state, major river, or mountain range is named Dixie. Yet everyone knows about this place. Ask any American and the answer will be that the South is Dixie. And if that person is a history buff, you'll be told that it's been that way since the Civil War. But why? Why is the South called Dixie?

There are several explanations. The most obvious refers to the Mason-Dixon Line, a border drawn in 1767 by two English surveyors, Charles Mason and Jeremiah Dixon, to settle a dispute between Pennsylvania and Maryland. After Pennsylvania abolished slavery in 1781, the Mason-Dixon Line became a general term for the border between the free and slave states. The southern side, or "Dixon's land," eventually morphed into "Dixieland." This makes sense. But you have to wonder why Southerners would want to use the name of an Englishman who never lived among them.

Maybe we should try following the money. Follow it all the way down to New Orleans in the early 1800s, and you'll find ten-dollar bills printed with the French word *dix* ("ten," pronounced "deece") being paid to planters who sold their cotton in the market. (The Louisiana Creole favored French money, so the Citizens Bank of Louisiana printed money with American currency denominations on one side and French denominations on the other.) Ten dollars was a lot of money in those days, and planters who made a big sale would brag about the number of "dixies" they raked in. As they couldn't speak French, they came down hard on the x, and Dixie was born. Soon, any place where this highly desirable currency circulated became known as Dixieland.

Even so, the name might have faded into history, except for Ohio-born Yankee songwriter Dan Emmett. In 1859, he published a banjo ditty called "I Wish I Was in Dixie." The song became quite popular on the minstrel circuit. Though it was reportedly a big favorite of none other than Abraham Lincoln himself, Southerners readily embraced it as their unofficial anthem during the Civil War.

Because of its connections with slavery and blackface minstrel shows, many people today feel that Dixieland has racist connotations. Some historians, however, believe that Emmett got the song from two African American musicians, Ben and Lew Snowden, with whom he occasionally performed in Ohio, making Dixie part of the black as well as white tradition. Recently, a few jazz musicians have begun to explore this idea, mixing the tune with black gospel and blues. After all, what was good enough for Abraham Lincoln should be good enough for the rest of us, too.

Q. If New Hampshire is in the U.S., where's Old Hampshire?

A. In 1622, colonial entrepreneurs Captain John Mason and Sir Ferdinando Gorges received a land grant from the Council for New England for all the territory between the Merrimack and Kennebec rivers.

In 1629, the two men split the grant, with Mason's share covering the land south of the Piscataqua River.

Mason named his area New Hampshire, after the English county of Hampshire, a place where he had spent much of his youth. And compared with New Hampshire, the original Hampshire is indeed old. Located on the south coast of England, it was first settled in Neolithic, or early prehistoric, times. Today, Hampshire is bordered by the counties of Wiltshire and Dorset to the west, Berkshire to the north, and West Sussex and Surrey to the east. The county's southern coastline is bounded by the Solent, a strait of the English Channel whose coast is renowned for historic castles, unspoiled nature preserves, and chichi yachting. Hampshire is among the largest nonmetropolitan counties, or shires, in England.

Q. How did California get its name?

A. Scholars believe it came from an early 16th-century work of fiction. *Las Sergas de Esplandian* by Ordonez de Montalvo tells the story of a force of Amazons led by Queen Calafia of the island of California, which was described as being near the Terrestrial Paradise, an island overflowing with gold. Many early Spanish explorers came to the New World in search of such a paradise, and for a short time they thought they might have found it in California.

Q. What was Alaska called before it was purchased by the United States?

A. Russian America. Russia sponsored expeditions to explore its northeastern corner, and in 1741, Captain Vitus Bering sited the Alaska mainland. Russian holdings in North America included settlements as far south as California and in the Hawaiian Islands, but Russia never put forth a concerted effort to establish actual colonies.

Q. What state was the first to grant Christmas legal status?

A. Christmas is an international holiday, but Alabama was the first state to grant it legal status.

It's commonly believed that Christmas has been a legal holiday in the United States since the nation was established, but that's not correct. While the birth of Christ has been celebrated worldwide for nearly two millennia, no mention of it appears anywhere in the establishing documents created by our country's founders.

As a result, it wasn't until 1836 that Christmas was finally granted legal recognition in the United States. The first state to do so? Alabama!

By 1890, all the remaining states and territories, plus the District of Columbia, had followed Alabama's lead in establishing Christmas as a legal holiday. Interestingly,

Christmas is also the only religious holiday to receive this kind of official secular recognition in America.

No cause for celebration
Despite this historic first step, Alabama celebrates Christmas pretty much like all the other states; nothing special is done to observe the Yellowhammer State's foresight in making Christmas something more than just a religious observance. But that shouldn't stop those who know about the first-of-its-kind legislation from feeling just a little superior.

The Christmas holiday aside, Alabama has hosted many other important achievements over the years. Among them:

- Alabama introduced Mardi Gras to the Western world. (Sorry, New Orleans!)

- Montgomery established the nation's first electric trolley system. It premiered in 1886.

- Dr. Luther Leonidas Hill of Montgomery performed the first open-heart surgery in the Western Hemisphere in 1902. He saved a boy's life by suturing a stab wound in the youngster's heart.

Q. **Why is Kansas City in Missouri and Missouri City in Texas?**

A. In the vast expanse that is the United States, quite a few cities and towns have the names of outside states. How about Virginia City, Nevada; Colorado City, Arizona; and Michigan City, Indiana? Pretty unimaginative—and confusing—huh?

In the case of Kansas City, Missouri, the town officially claimed the Kansas name before the state existed. In 1838, John Calvin McCoy, regarded as the father of Kansas City, and thirteen other men bought 271 acres of land known as the Gabriel Prudhomme farm. This property would become Kansas City's first downtown district, but first the men needed to agree on a name for their new township. According to legend, the owners considered several names, including Port Fonda, Rabbitville, and Possum Trot. In the end, they settled on Kansas, for the Kansa Indians who inhabited the area.

Kansas, Missouri, was chartered as a town on June 1, 1850, and as a city on February 22, 1853. In 1854, the Kansas-Nebraska Act established the boundaries of a large territory to the west, which was also given the name Kansas. The territory of Kansas became the 34th state in 1861. In 1889, the Missouri city known as Kansas officially changed its name to Kansas City to distinguish itself from Kansas the state.

As for how Missouri City came to be in Texas, that was a matter of marketing. In 1890, a few real-estate developers from Houston bought four acres of land near the BBB&C railroad. In an effort to draw settlers from the North to their new railroad, farming, and ranching town, the developers named the area Missouri City and launched an advertising campaign in St. Louis, Missouri.

Missouri City was touted as "a land of genial sunshine and eternal summer." Despite the developers' creative flourishes, most of Missouri City's initial settlers came from Arlington, Texas, in the Dallas-Fort Worth area, in 1894. When a wave of settlers from the North did make it down to Missouri City the following year, they were greeted by a harsh blizzard that included 28 inches of snow.

Q. What are the state nicknames for the South?

A.

- Alabama has no official nickname, but it has been called "The Cotton State," and "Heart of Dixie" has appeared on state license plates.

- In 1995 Arkansas officially changed its nickname from "Land of Opportunity" to "The Natural State."

- The nickname for Florida is "The Sunshine State." It was first used on license plates in 1949, but the state legislature didn't make it official until 1970.

- Georgia is another state that has no nickname officially assigned by the state legislature, but it is frequently known as "The Peach State" and "The Empire State of the South."

- Kentucky's nickname is "The Bluegrass State."

- Louisiana gets its nickname, "The Pelican State," from its state bird, the brown pelican.

- Mississippi's state flower is the magnolia, which is why many call it "The Magnolia State."

- North Carolina has been called "The Old North State," on account of it being older and further north than South Carolina, and "The Tar Heel State." Although the state's pine forests provided an early tar industry, the origin of the second name is uncertain. One popular tale tells of North Carolinian soldiers in the Civil War who held their position while other retreated, due to the tar on the heels.

- South Carolina is called "The Palmetto State," after the palmetto tree, which also appears on the state flag.

- Tennessee is "The Volunteer State," a name it got received when Tennesseans enthusiastically answered their governor's call for volunteers to fight the British in the War of 1812.

- Virginia, as the first of the British colonies to be established in the New World, is called "The Old Dominion."

- West Virginia calls itself "The Mountain State."

Q. What are some myths about the Civil War?

A. There's a certain romance to the tales that have circulated in the almost 150 years since the Civil War. Many are true, but many others are laced with falsehoods. At the risk of bursting some American history bubbles, here is a sampling of the myths swirling around the Civil War.

Myth: The Civil War was America's first disagreement over slavery.

The Founders of the United States had been concerned with the ownership of slaves, particularly as it played out in the issue of states' rights, since the Articles of Confederation were ratified in 1781. A confederation, by definition, is a loose alignment of states, each with the power to self-regulate. The Southern states favored slavery, and every time the issue of states' rights emerged on the national front, the South would threaten secession.

Other landmark congressional acts and court judgments that influenced slavery in America before the Civil War include the Three-Fifths Compromise in the Constitution, the Missouri Compromise of 1820, the Compromise of 1850, the Kansas-Nebraska Act, and the Dred Scott Decision.

Myth: The Emancipation Proclamation freed all the slaves in America.

Lincoln wrote the edict in September 1862, and it went into effect on January 1, 1863. The language of the document was clear: Any slave that was still held in the states that had seceded from the Union was "forever free" as of January 1, 1863.

Significantly, this edict did not include border states in which slaves were still held, such as Kentucky or Missouri, because Lincoln didn't want to stoke rebellion there. As one might expect, the Southern states paid hardly any attention to the announcement by the Union president. They'd already turned their backs on him and his nation, and as far as they were concerned, the Union president held no power over them.

Myth: The Union soldiers firmly believed in the cause of freeing the slaves.

For the most part, the soldiers had little, if any, opinion on slavery. At first, many young men enlisted in the Union army as a romantic adventure. Early opinion estimated that the war would end within a few months, and many decided they could afford that much time away from their work, school, or home life.

Myth: The South's secession was the first time in American history a state tried to leave the Union.

During the War of 1812, New England almost seceded in order to protect its trade with Great Britain. In the 1850s, President James Buchanan, who held office immediately before Abraham Lincoln, stated the federal government would not resort to force to prevent secession. In 1869, four years after the end of the war, the Supreme Court declared the act of state secession to be unconstitutional.

Myth: The Confederate attack on Fort Sumter was the first act of Southern aggression against Northern targets.

The attack on Fort Sumter was preceded by attacks on other forts and military installations in Confederate territory. On January 9, 1861, Mississippi followed South Carolina to become the second state to secede from the Union. Within a week, Mississippi's governor ordered an armed battery placed on the bluff above the wharf at Vicksburg. His declared intention was to force Union vessels to stop to be searched—after all, it was rumored that a cannon had been sent to a Baton Rouge arsenal. Intentions aside, the fact is the battery actually fired on a number of vessels in order to make them come about, including the *Gladiator*, the *Imperial*, and the *A. O. Tyler*.

Prior to this incident, the Confederate Congress had approved the creation of a volunteer army of 100,000 soldiers—far larger than any military force that was intended strictly for keeping the peace would presumably need to be.

Myth: Abraham Lincoln wrote his Gettysburg Address on the back of an envelope while riding the train on his way to make the speech.

Lincoln would never have waited until the last minute to write such an important oration, which was part of the consecration of the Gettysburg Cemetery in November 1863. But even if he had, the train ride itself would have prevented legible writing. The 1860s-period train cars bounced, swayed, and made horseback riding seem smooth by comparison. Several drafts of the Gettysburg Address (including what is referred to as the "reading draft") have been archived at the Library of Congress and other academic institutions. They are written—very legibly—on lined paper and Executive Mansion stationery.

Q. What was the Trail of Tears?

A. In 1830, the U.S. Congress passed the Indian Removal Act, which forced the resettlement of most Cherokee from their homes in the southeastern United States to land west of the Mississippi River. Those Cherokee who refused to go were arrested by the U.S. Army between 1838 and 1839 and sent to an area that was then called "Indian Territory" (now Oklahoma). Of the 15,000 Cherokee who set out on the journey, more than 4,000 died along the way. Edward Wilkerson Bushyhead was seven years old when he moved with his family. Later in his life, he traveled to California, where he became a sheriff, then served as chief of police, and eventually owned a newspaper. When he died at age 75 in 1907, he was believed to be the last survivor of the Trail of Tears.

Q. What were the Zoot Suit Riots?

A. A volatile mix of hot summer nights, angry sailors, and ethnic tension in Southern California during World War II could only lead to an explosion.

The country was abuzz with wartime pressure and a fresh surge of racial tension in 1943. World War II was in full swing, and Los Angeles was flooded with sailors. They spilled out of local naval bases into a city already filled to the brim. Added to the heap of an overpopulated city came the self-described *pachucos* (a word that has its origins in a slang term for residents of El Paso, Texas). Pachucos, decked out in distinctive full zoot-suit garb and ducktail 'dos, had been seen around town for years and had fostered a reputation for stirring up trouble. This "trouble" was often the product of an anti-Latino bias that circulated through the streets of LA among residents and law enforcement officials alike. With the addition of so many military personnel to the city, the blend of diversity and testosterone proved to be violent.

An Unfamiliar Culture
Prior to their Los Angeles experience with Mexican Americans, the era's military personnel typically possessed little experience with the flamboyantly represented Latino culture they now found in their midst. The hue of pachucos' skin differentiated them from the white masses, but their telltale garb really jabbed at the restless forces. The ostentatious jewelry, prominently wide-brimmed hats, and elaborately tapered pants earmarked the pachucos as the "troublemaking" Zoot Suiters.

Despite the pachucos' cartoonish costumes, many Los Angelinos believed that there were good reasons for the masses to fear their presence. With their infiltration of Los Angeles came a rash of gang activity, and a mysterious but much-publicized gang-related death made headlines in 1942. These events served to perpetuate the public cries of the zoot-suit-menace mania that was already striking the area. All this racially laced trepidation came to a head in the summer of 1943.

The Mob Attacks
Based on claims of a pachuco-prompted altercation, a group of sailors initiated retaliation on a grand and vindictive scale. On June 3, 1943, a group of sailors embarked on an incursion into the barrios of East LA. Armed with belts, clubs, and chains, the assemblage was out for blood.

Although pachucos were typically clad in zoot suits, not all zoot-suit-adorned Mexican Americans were part of the pachuco group. That made no difference to the sailors, however. No Latino male was safe. Zoot-suit wearers were the initial targets, but soon the sailors found any East LA resident fair game. Zoot suit or not, any Mexican American man who crossed the mob's path was made victim of the angry onslaught. Worse yet, women were raped, and even the occasional African American and Filipino American to happen onto the scene was attacked by the mob.

But Who's Responsible?

To add insult to injury, at the end of the days-long attack, a collective of mostly Mexican Americans was charged with the illegalities. While hundreds of Mexican Americans were arrested, a mere nine sailors were taken into custody. Of those nine, only one was deemed guilty—and just of a small-time crime.

The *Los Angeles Times* marked its approval of this discrimination with a headline that declared "Zoot Suiters Learn Lesson in Fight with Servicemen." The implication of the article was that the menacing Mexicans were simply out of control. The national press picked up the story and reported a similar version of the tale in other cities. In outrage, or perhaps in a frenzy of the racially tense excitement overtaking the nation, copycat riots emerged across the United States. In response to the fracas, the U.S. military ordered all personnel to keep away from the streets of Los Angeles in an effort to settle the unrest. Of course, in one last jab at the pachucos, an ordinance was passed in Los Angeles that declared the wearing of zoot suits illegal.

Q. Were there civilian casualties at Pearl Harbor?

A. While the largest loss of life at Pearl Harbor on December 7, 1941, occurred when the forward magazine on the battleship USS *Arizona* exploded, a forgotten fact about the "Day of Infamy" is that at least 48 civilians also lost their lives.

The Japanese attack on U.S. naval forces at Pearl Harbor began on December 7, 1941, at 7:53 A.M. Hawaiian time. By 9:00 radio stations throughout the island urged civilians to "get off the roads and stay off . . . don't block traffic . . . stay at home."

Friendly fire was a major cause of American casualties. Thirty-two civilians were killed in the city of Honolulu. The largest group was killed on the corner of Kukui Street and Nuuanu Avenue. Jitsuo Hirasaki, his three children, and their cousin all died when an antiaircraft shell exploded on top of their family-run restaurant. Seven restaurant patrons also died.

The second largest loss of civilian life came at the intersection of Judd and Iholena streets. Joseph Adams, his son John, Joseph's brother-in-law Joseph McCabe Sr., and McCabe's nephew David Kahookele had just attended Catholic Mass and were on their way home when they heard a radio announcement asking all shipyard workers to report for work. The men were killed en route to Pearl Harbor when an antiaircraft shell hit their car. Twelve-year-old Matilda Faufata was killed by shrapnel from the explosion while standing in her front doorway.

On Kamanaiki Street in north Honolulu, a family of four was killed in their house by an exploding shell. Shrapnel killed sisters Barbara and Gertrude Ornellas. Gertrude was standing on the front porch and Barbara was in her bedroom. The girls' uncle, Peter Lopes, and family member Frank Ohashi also lost their lives.

Hayako Ohta, her three-month-old daughter Janet, and the baby's aunt Kiyoko died when a shell hit their building on the corner of King and McCully streets.

Patrick Chong and his seven-month-old daughter Eunice Wilson were killed when a shell exploded near their house on Leilehua Lane. Nineteen-year-old Edward Kondo died in the same area, while several of his family members were wounded.

Torao Migita, a private with D Company, 298th Infantry Regiment stationed at Schofield Barracks, was the only Japanese-American serviceman to die on December 7. Migita was on a weekend pass when he was killed in downtown Honolulu.

Ten civilians died in various rural locations on Oahu including Wahiawa, Waipahu, Pearl City, Red Hill, Ewa, John Rodger Airport, and the Kaheohe Bay Naval Air Station.

The greatest loss of civilian life outside of Honolulu occurred at Hickam Air Force Base. Three members of the Honolulu Fire Department—Captain John Carreira, Thomas Macy, and Harry Pang—were killed when a Japanese bomb exploded in the hanger where they were fighting fires. Two other civilians died at Hickam.

Despite the fact Japanese planes strafed targets after dropping their payload, only one civilian was killed in this manner. Daniel LaVerne, a defense worker at Red Hill, died late on December 10 after being hit by bullets from a Japanese plane.

According to the 1940 census, 160,000 Hawaiian residents were of Japanese descent. A large mix of Korean, Chinese, and Filipino descendants also called the islands home. While official estimates of civilians killed on December 7 ranges from 48 to 68, the great majority of those killed were of Asian-Pacific descent. Just as the young men of America's military had their lives taken from them that fateful Sunday morning, so too did a group of largely forgotten Hawaiian civilians.

Q. Who was Dorie Miller?

A. Doris "Dorie" Miller, so named because his mom's midwife had expected a girl, stood that early December 1941 morning on the deck of the USS *West Virginia*. Trained as a cook, no one would have thought he'd emerge from Pearl Harbor as a hero.

December 7, 1941
Twenty-year-old "Dorie" Miller joined the navy in September 1939. He enrolled at the recruiting post in his hometown of Waco, Texas, after taking a ride in the back of the bus with a group of other black recruits. Blacks in the navy were then restricted to kitchen duty. So when he enrolled, Miller became a mess attendant, eventually working his way up to ship's cook.

On an otherwise sleepy Sunday, Miller watched as an array of aircraft drew near. Two sections of the squadron dove toward the harbor and the airfield at adjacent Ford Island. Alongside his ship, the *West Virginia*, was the battleship *Tennessee*. Along the quays forward were the *Maryland* and the *Oklahoma*, and to the stern was the *Arizona*. Unlike most of the crew, Miller was on duty that morning, collecting officers' laundry. Although barred from a combat post because of his race, he had proved himself a fighter—he was the *West Virginia*'s heavyweight boxing champ.

It was odd, Miller thought, that aircraft were training so close to a naval and air base. Then four of the planes dove toward Ford Island. Suddenly, the airport's hangar and a clutch of Devastor dive-bombers on the runways exploded. Miller later recalled, "I found myself an unwilling occupant of a front-row seat from which to witness the proceedings."

Miller watched another group of planes, rising suns on their wings, veer down toward the *West Virginia*, and drop five 18-inch-wide torpedoes into the waves. Within seconds, the ship shuddered and heaved from massive explosions. Soon after, Japanese planes dropped two armor-piercing bombs into the battleship, sparking massive fires.

The ship's communications officer pressed Miller into action—the captain was bleeding badly and had to be moved. Miller and the officer made a nightmarish journey through the dark, smoke-filled corridors of the vessel. En route, Miller felt a gigantic explosion—not from the *West Virginia*, as it turned out, but from the nearby USS *Arizona*, which had blown up, taking the lives of 1,177 men. Employing his strength as a boxer and an ex-high-school fullback, Miller helped hoist the gravely injured captain to the forecastle, and later to the bridge.

Back on deck, Miller saw the ship was listing; water poured over the side. Just ahead, Miller could see the now-capsized hull of the *Oklahoma*. He pulled wounded sailors on the main deck to the relative safety of the quarterdeck. Miller and Lieutenant Commander Frederic White then turned to a half-dozen survivors bobbing in the fiery, oily waters alongside their battleship. He and White tossed out ropes, hauled the sailors aboard, and then collapsed from exhaustion. However, the force of 181 Japanese aircraft continued their bombing and strafing runs.

Miller and White rushed to a pair of Browning .50-caliber antiaircraft machine guns. Even as a cook, Miller had been trained for combat, but not specifically in the use of antiaircraft guns. He put his training in gear. "The sky seemed filled with diving planes and the black bursts of exploding antiaircraft shells," he remembered. He tracked a swooping Japanese plane through the gun sight, his thumbs squeezing the firing levers. Smoke billowed out of the aircraft. Seconds later, it crashed, throwing up a great plume of water from the embattled harbor.

"It wasn't hard," Miller stated. "I just pulled the trigger and she worked fine. I had watched the others with these guns. I guess I fired her for about 15 minutes." As the attackers tried to finish off the U.S. Pacific Fleet, Miller and a few other gunners battled back. Finally, the *West Virginia* settled into the shallow harbor, with 130 of its 1,541-man crew killed. Miller and other survivors swung over by rope to the waiting *Tennessee*.

Stateside Recognition

Word spread back to the mainland about Miller's Pearl Harbor heroism. The *Pittsburgh Courier*, a prominent black newspaper, campaigned to have the sailor decorated. And in May 1942, Admiral Chester W. Nimitz, commander of the Pacific Fleet, stood on the aircraft carrier USS *Enterprise* and personally awarded Miller the Navy Cross, the service's third-highest decoration. Said Nimitz: "This marks the first time in this conflict that such high tribute has been made in the Pacific Fleet to a member of his race and I'm sure that the future will see others similarly honored for brave acts." Capitalizing on Miller's fame, the navy sent him stateside on a war-bonds tour, with stops in his hometown of Waco, in Dallas, and at Chicago's Great Lakes Naval Training Center, which had begun training blacks for positions more responsible than mess attendant.

Dorie Returns to Service

One more war mission awaited Miller. He was onboard the escort carrier USS *Liscome Bay*, whose planes supported the bloody but successful November 1943 invasion of Tarawa atoll. As the invasion fleet was readying to leave the area, the Japanese submarine I-175 struck the carrier. Its torpedo ignited the magazine and practically tore off the vessel's stern where Miller was manning an antiaircraft gun. He was most likely killed instantly (though not officially presumed dead until a year and a day later). Three hundred seventy-three of his fellow 646 crewmen were also killed.

Miller's courage against the enemy and against the racial codes of the day had great effect. In February 1944, the navy commissioned its first black officers, and in 1948, President Truman formally integrated all branches of the U.S. armed services. A final legacy of Miller's was the commissioning in 1973 of the Knox-class frigate the USS *Miller*, named in his honor. The *Miller* saw service in the Persian Gulf, Black Sea, and elsewhere.

Actor Cuba Gooding Jr. played the part of Dorie Miller in the 2001 film *Pearl Harbor*.

Q. Where did the Quartering Act of 1765 allow British troops to sleep?

A. In colonists' homes. This was one of what colonists considered "The Intolerable Acts" that brought about the Revolution. In New York City in 1766, 1,500 British troops were refused quarter and forced to remain on their ships. The Founders felt so strongly about the act of quartering, as a matter of fact, that they limited it in the Bill of Rights. In its entirety, the Third Amendment to the U.S. Constitution reads: "No Soldier shall, in time of peace be quartered in any house, without the consent of the Owner, nor in time of war, but in a manner to be prescribed by law."

Q. What was the Haymarket Riot?

A. What began as a campaign for an eight-hour workday ended with a bloody event Chicago will never forget.

It was the mid-1880s, and Chicago was in a state of transition. Industry was growing more and more mechanized—good news for the corporations that were able to increase profits and lower wages, but bad news for workers who were putting in 12 to 14 grueling hours a day, 6 miserable days a week. In October 1884, the Federation of Organized Trade and Labor Unions set a goal to make the eight-hour workday standard, even if nationwide strikes were necessary to make that goal a reality. The stage was set.

The Calm Before the Storm

On May 1, 1886, hundreds of thousands of workers across the country took to the streets in support of an eight-hour workday. The first few days of the strike were relatively peaceful, but all hell broke loose on May 3, when police killed several unarmed strikers near Chicago's McCormick Reaper Works.

Workers gathered in a light rain in Haymarket Square on the West Side on May 4. Mayor Carter Harrison Sr. stopped by in a show of support for the workers, and then left early when it appeared that all was peaceful. The rest, as they say, is history—and a somewhat murky history at that, as many questions remain about what unfolded in the incident now known as the Haymarket Riot.

Every Man for Himself

Once the mayor left, the police inspector sent in the riot police to disperse the crowd. At the same time, a bomb blasted the ranks of the police force. The police opened fire. Workers reportedly returned fire. A few short minutes later, eight policemen were dead, and scores of workers and bystanders had been injured. The *Chicago Tribune* later quoted an unnamed police officer, who reported, "a very large number of the police were wounded by each other's revolvers . . . It was every man for himself, and while some got two or three squares away, the rest emptied their revolvers, mainly into each other."

The Fallout

Chicago police immediately swept across the city in search of the bomber. They arrested eight known anarchists (August Spies, Samuel Fielden, Oscar Neebe, Michael Schwab, Louis Lingg, George Engel, Adolph Fischer, and Albert Parsons) and charged them with the crime. After a well-publicized trial, the jury (which included a Marshall Field's sales rep and not a single industrial worker) returned guilty verdicts for all eight, even though only two of the men were even at the Haymarket the night of the incident. The men had clearly been tried for their incendiary speeches leading up to the Haymarket incident, not for anything they had actually done. Seven of the men were sentenced to death, and the show trial resulted in protests around the world.

Seriously, Who Threw the Bomb?

Spies, Fischer, Engel, and Parsons were hanged on November 11, 1887; Lingg had committed suicide in prison one day earlier. Governor Altgeld pardoned Schwab, Fielden, and Neebe in 1893. To the present day, no one is sure who threw the bomb, but most historians believe it was one of two anarchists who were present at the protest that day: Rudolph Schnaubelt or George Meng—neither of whom was ever arrested for the crime.

Historians consider Haymarket one of the seminal events in the history of labor, and its legacy resonates to this day. The Haymarket defendants stand as icons of the American labor movement and are remembered with rallies, parades, and speeches around the world on the anniversary of the bombing. But most important is the spirit of assembly that can be traced back to Haymarket. Today, monuments stand at the corner of Des Plaines and Randolph streets (near the spot where the bomb was thrown) and in Forest Park, Illinois, at the grave of Spies, Fischer, Engel, Parsons, and Lingg. These symbols are poignant reminders of Chicago's critical place in labor history.

Q. Where was the headquarters for the Manhattan Project?

A. Although the Manhattan Project is often associated with Los Alamos, New Mexico, it actually had major facilities there and at two other sites: Oak Ridge, Tennessee, and Hanford, Washington. Each site was to have a different function. Oak Ridge was to refine uranium-235 using an enormous

electromagnet. Hanford, chosen for proximity to the Columbia River's limitless supply of cooling water, raced to build a reactor capable of making plutonium-239. Los Alamos figured out how to build the fissile material into bombs.

Q. What happened at Kent State University on May 4, 1970?

A. Many people know about the tragic shootings at Kent State, but few know the full story, which was obscured by inaccurate media reports and protracted legal proceedings against the National Guardsmen involved. During a campus demonstration at Kent State University (KSU) on May 4, 1970, members of the Ohio National Guard shot and killed four students and wounded nine others. To fully understand the reasons behind the tragedy, it's crucial to know the historical context.

Located in Northeast Ohio, KSU was one of several universities organizing and protesting against President Richard Nixon's expansion of the Vietnam War. Richard Nixon had been elected president in 1968, partly on the promise that he would end the Vietnam War.

In early 1969, the president took a few steps to decrease United States involvement in Southeast Asia, but on April 30, 1970, he approved a massive military operation in Cambodia. Antiwar protests were planned on many college campuses, which angered Nixon, who referred to protesters as "bums."

State of Emergency

On May 1, an antiwar rally was held at Kent State, with plans for another rally on May 4. Many young people created a disturbance in downtown Kent that night, committing acts of vandalism and frightening citizens. Business owners blamed KSU students, but witnesses observed that outsiders—including a motorcycle gang and other nonstudents—were among those making trouble.

Police used tear gas to disperse the crowd, and Mayor Leroy Stanton declared a state of emergency. This allowed Governor James Rhodes to approve a request for the National Guard.

On May 2, the Reserve Officers' Training Corps (ROTC) building, an old structure scheduled for razing, went up in flames. Although the arsonists were never identified, the press and townspeople blamed the protesters. Demonstrators openly confronted police and hampered the firefighters who came to extinguish the flames by cutting hoses and throwing rocks.

Though guardsmen were stationed all over campus on May 3, everything remained relatively quiet until Governor Rhodes held a press conference that evening. He warned that he would use force to stop the demonstrators, declaring them the "worst type of people we harbor in America" and comparing them to fascists, vigilantes, and communists. New clashes between the protesters and law enforcement broke the calm with rocks and tear gas.

The Right to Dissent

On May 4, the university attempted to ban the rally, but by noon, a crowd of 1,500 people, from avid antiwar radicals to passive spectators, had gathered. Students felt they had a right to hold a rally, and the presence of the guardsmen fostered resentment.

About 100 young, inexperienced National Guardsmen in riot gear armed with M-1 rifles stood on the edge of the Commons. When General Robert Canterbury ordered the demonstrators to end the rally and disperse, police and guardsmen drove across the Commons to push the crowd forward and out of the way.

One particular group of National Guardsmen—their bayonets fixed—followed some students to the top of Blanket Hill, where those students dispersed. Then about a dozen guardsmen turned around and shot down the hill in the direction of the other demonstrators and students. Some fired in the air and into the ground, while others shot directly into the crowd.

More than 60 shots were fired, killing four students and wounding nine. Those killed were Allison Krause, Sandra Scheuer, Jeffrey Miller, and William Schroeder. The guardsmen retreated to the Commons, where angry students confronted them. A handful of faculty members and student leaders diffused the situation.

The school was closed, and students were ordered to leave campus. These shootings galvanized 4.3 million participants to protest the war on 500 college campuses around the country. State and federal investigations were launched, with criminal and civil charges brought against some of the guardsmen. In 1970, President Nixon's own Commission on Campus Unrest concluded that the "indiscriminate firing of rifles into a crowd of students and the deaths that followed were unnecessary, unwarranted, and inexcusable." However, none of the guards were convicted or punished, partly due to interference from Governor Rhodes.

Aftermath
Character assassinations of the dead and wounded students followed, which were spread to the press and circulated among top officials in Washington, with FBI Director J. Edgar Hoover calling one of the victims "nothing more than a whore." The jury in a 1975 civil trial ruled that none of the guardsmen were legally responsible for the deaths and injuries, but the judge ordered a new trial when it was discovered that one of the jurors had been threatened. All legal action around the KSU shootings ended in January 1979 with a $675,000 settlement for the victims. The National Guard signed a statement of regret but emphasized that it was not an apology. The memory of the four students continues to endure in the country's mind, far beyond the borders of Ohio.

Q. Can you serve in the U.S. military if you have flat feet?

A. It may sound like an urban legend started by draft dodgers, but it isn't. If you have *pes planus* (flat feet), you can't serve in the U.S. military.

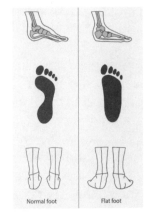

Normal foot   Flat foot

Pes planus is a condition in which the longitudinal arch in the foot, which runs from the heel to the ball, has flattened out or never developed normally. The condition can be genetic. It also can result from a malady such as diabetes, a stroke, rheumatoid arthritis, or a foot injury. Even through many people who have flat feet rarely have symptoms or problems beyond foot pain, the U.S. military does not want anything to do with an archless individual.

Documentation on the subject from the U.S. Army, issued December 14, 2007, states: "Current symptomatic *pes planus* (acquired (734) or congenital (754.6)) or history of *pes planus* corrected by prescription or custom orthotics is disqualifying." Translation: Even if your flat feet are under control with shoe inserts, you still can't be all that you can be.

Other foot-related maladies that prevent one from joining the U.S. military are hammer toes, overriding toes, clubfoot, ingrown toenails, and/or toe deformities. Why? Easy. These conditions may prevent a soldier from wearing military footwear properly, thus impairing walking, running, marching, and jumping. The U.S. armed forces has no room for, "Hup, two, three, *ouch!*"

Q. What was Molly Pitcher's true identity?

A. Historians disagree about Molly—not over whether she lived, but over her true identity. Did a cannon-cocker's wife truly step up and serve a gun under fire in the American Revolution?

Was Molly Pitcher real?
A couple of Revolutionary women's stories sound a lot like Molly's. Because women have "pitched in" during battle in nearly every war, that's neither surprising nor a revelation. It wasn't rare in that era for wives to accompany

their husbands on military duty, to say nothing of those daring few women who masqueraded as men.

Who was Molly?

Many historians say she was an Irish immigrant named Mary Hays (later McCauly). Some believe that Molly was Margaret Corbin, a Pennsylvania native. The most likely case is that both were real women and that the legend of Molly Pitcher commingles the two.

What did Mary Hays do?

The story, likely accurate, credits her first with bringing water (the "pitcher" part explained) to the artillery gunners at the Battle of Monmouth (1778).

It wasn't just drinking water. A soldier had to wet-sponge a cannon after a shot in order to douse any residual embers. If he or she didn't, the person pushing in the next powder charge would suffer the consequences. Accounts describe Mary as a woman who was always ready with a choice profanity and was as brave as any man, and she is widely credited with evacuating wounded men.

And Margaret Corbin?

Margaret Corbin's tale enters focus at the Battle of Fort Washington (1776) and has her first helping her husband crew a cannon, then firing it unassisted after his death in action. (That would be possible, but very slow.) Taken out of action by grapeshot—a cannon firing musket balls as a super shotgun—she was evacuated and given a military pension by the Continental government. Considering said government's notorious poverty and lousy credit, there's doubt whether poor Margaret ever collected any money in time to help her.

The name Molly Pitcher later became a generic term used to refer to women who carried water to men on the battlefield during the Revolutionary War.

Q. How did escaped slaves travel the Underground Railroad?

A. The very mention of the Underground Railroad reaches deep into the American psyche, invoking images of daring midnight escapes, secret tunnels, and concealed doors, as well as the exploits of thousands of daring men and women.

The story of American slaves seeking escape from their masters long predates the invention of the railroad and its associated terms. Even before the Underground Railroad, escapees were often aided by individuals or organizations opposed to the institution of slavery.

The Fugitive Slave Acts

As the United States careened toward civil war, the arguments between supporters of slavery and opponents became increasingly heated. Northern states began abolishing slavery on an individual basis—and became instant magnets for those fleeing servitude. In response, Congress passed Fugitive Slave Acts in 1793 and 1850, rendering escaped slaves fugitives for life, eligible for return to bondage on nothing more than the word of a white man. Any constable who refused to apprehend runaway slaves was fined. With the Northern states thus a less attractive final destination, runaways headed to Canada, where slavery had been outlawed in 1834.

Meanwhile, abolitionist societies began to spring up, though a surprising number of them supported the return of escaped slaves to their masters, believing they could end the practice through moral persuasion rather than by violating the law.

All Aboard

Despite hesitation on the part of some abolitionist societies, however, there were always individuals and groups who were sympathetic to the cause of the runaway slave and willing to place themselves at risk to help slaves find freedom. These benefactors ranged from white citizens to free blacks to other slaves willing to risk being beaten or sold for giving aid to runaways. Often, these protectors acted alone with little more than a vague idea of where to send a fugitive slave other than in the general direction of north. When a sympathetic individual discovered a runaway, he or she would often simply do what seemed best at the moment, whether that meant providing food and clothing, throwing pursuers off the track, or giving the runaway slave a wagon ride to the next town.

By the 1840s, the expansion of the railroad was having a major impact on American society, and abolitionist activists quickly adopted its terminology. Conductors were those people who helped their passengers—runaway slaves—onto the next station or town, where they made contact with a stationmaster—the person in charge of the local organization. The most famous conductor, Harriet Tubman, was herself an escaped slave who risked no less than 19 trips back into slave country to aid family members and others.

In some areas, small cells sprang up in which each person knew only about a contact on the next farm or in the next town, perhaps with the nebulous goal of somehow sending escapees into the care of well-known abolitionist societies in far-off Philadelphia or Boston. The image of one overriding national organization guiding the effort is largely a misleading one, but it was one encouraged by both abolitionists and slaveholders. The abolitionists were not hesitant to play up the romantic railroad imagery in an effort to bolster their fund-raising efforts. Their descriptions were so vivid that Frederick Douglass himself suggested they cease talking about it, lest they reveal their methods to their enemies. Likewise, Southern plantation owners were quick to play up the reports as proof that there was a vast abolitionist conspiracy bent on robbing them of their legal investment in slaves. As a result, some slave owners in border states converted their slaves to cash— selling them to the Deep South rather than risking their escape— a fate many slaves considered nothing less than a death sentence.

Efforts at undermining the institution of slavery did exist but were scarcely clandestine. Many abolitionists were quite open about their intentions.

"Devils and good people, walking in the road at the same time"

Despite the presence of Underground Railroad workers, the experience of a runaway slave was never anything other than harsh. On striking out for freedom, even successful escapees faced an ordeal that could last months. During their journey, they rarely had food, shelter, or appropriate clothing. Every white face was a potential enemy, as were some of their fellow black people, who were sometimes employed as decoys to help catch runaways. A false Underground Railroad even existed. Participants would take a runaway in and promise him safe passage only to deliver him to the local slave market. Often the escapees had no idea where they were going or the distance to be covered.

Although estimates vary wildly, one widely reported figure is that approximately 100,000 slaves found freedom either through their own initiative or with the aid of the Underground Railroad before the rest of those in bondage were freed during and after the Civil War. The history of the Underground Railroad was largely written decades after the fact, and it is occasionally hard to separate reliable facts from the aged recollections of those justifiably proud of their efforts at securing liberty for their fellow man.

Culture

Q. Who wrote the first American novel?

A. William Hill Brown wrote *The Power of Sympathy*, the first American novel, in 1789. Steeped in controversy, the plot of the novel—with its themes of seduction, incest, and suicide—would be more readily accepted in today's culture than it was in late 18th-century America.

Printer Isaiah Thomas was contracted to publish a limited run of the book and to sell it through his two bookshops. In an ironic twist—given the historical significance the book later assumed—*The Power of Sympathy* was presented as the work of an anonymous author.

Even if the book had been properly credited at the outset, few readers outside of upper-crust Boston would have been familiar with the author. When *The Power of Sympathy* appeared, William Hill Brown was a reasonably prolific but little-known playwright. He later wrote a comic opera, poetry, essays, and two more novels.

The son of a respected clockmaker, Brown was born in Boston in November 1765. He attended the Boston Boy's School, where he pursued creative writing, a craft encouraged by his step-aunt. Brown spent his formative years in an upper-class Boston neighborhood, living across the street from a married, politically active lawyer named Perez Morton.

In 1788, rumors of a romantic scandal involving Morton and his sister-in-law, Frances Apthorp, circulated among Boston's elite. The rumor turned out to be true, and rather than face public ridicule, the mortified Frances committed suicide. Perez, on the other hand, continued with his life as though nothing had happened. The public apparently went along with this tactic. Morton was later elected speaker of the lower house in the General Court of Massachusetts in 1806 and was named attorney general in 1810.

Writer (and former neighbor) William Brown was naturally well aware of the Morton-Apthorp scandal and published his book just a year later.

Following a novelistic style popular during the period, *The Power of Sympathy* unfolds via letters exchanged by central and secondary characters. The stinger is that the protagonists, Thomas Harrington and Harriot Fawcett, are about to unknowingly embark on an incestuous relationship.

In the novel, Harriot is Thomas's half-sister, born out of wedlock to a mistress of Thomas's father. For obvious reasons of propriety, the pregnancy and birth had been kept secret from the community and the rest of the family. When Harriot discovers the truth, she commits suicide. The facts soon become clear to Thomas as well, and he elects to follow his half-sister in suicide.

Credit Where Credit Is Due

Pressure from the Morton and Apthorp families, as well as from other prominent citizens, forced Brown to remove his book from circulation. Many copies were subsequently destroyed, and few exist today. In an odd twist, when the novel was reissued in the 19th century—nearly 100 years later—it was attributed to a deceased, once-popular Boston poet named Sarah Apthorp Morton, who happened to be the wife of Perez Morton—the man whose indiscretion helped inspire the novel in the first place! A correction issued by William Brown's aged niece not long after the book's republication led to proper attribution at last. Brown would finally be recognized as the author of the first novel written and published in America.

Q. Who's Oscar, and why is he associated with an Academy Award?

A. Oscar de la Renta. Oscar Madison. Oscar the Grouch. Famous Oscars all, but perhaps none is more recognizable than the 13.5-inch statuette that is handed out at the annual Academy Awards ceremony. Who is this golden boy, anyway?

Oscar looks like your everyday nude dude (albeit one who's non-anatomically correct), but he's actually a knight. He holds a crusader's sword and stands upon a film reel that has five spokes that represent the original branches of the Academy of Motion Picture Arts and Sciences: actors, writers, directors, producers, and technicians.

Why is he called Oscar instead of something befitting a knight, maybe Arthur or Geoffrey or Tristan? The question has sparked debate in Hollywood and beyond. One widely believed—though unsubstantiated—explanation is that the handle originated with former academy librarian Margaret Herrick. Around 1931, she is supposed to have commented that the statuette bore an uncanny resemblance to her uncle, a Texas farmer named Oscar Pierce. (Actually, he was her cousin.)

Another popular answer involves legendary actress Bette Davis. She is said to have named the Best Actress Academy Award she won in 1936 for her performance in *Dangerous* after her ex-husband, bandleader Harmon Oscar Nelson Jr. Apparently, Davis thought the backsides of Oscar the statuette and Oscar the bandleader were similarly shaped.

However the moniker came to be, it caught on quickly. The academy officially adopted it as the statuette's nickname in 1939, and few people today would know Oscar by his formal title—The Academy Award of Merit.

Q. The 1820 sinking of the *Essex* was the inspiration for which classic American novel?

A. The *Essex*, a Nantucket whaling ship that met an untimely end in the South Pacific after 15 months at sea, was the inspiration for Herman Melville's *Moby Dick*. The *Essex* met its fate when an enraged sperm whale rammed and sank the 238-ton ship.

Melville's novel ended when the ship went down, but that was just the beginning of the story for the 20 men who survived the whale's wrath in 1820. They spent months aboard three small boats and crossed more than 4,500 miles of ocean before they reached the South American coastline. Not all of the men survived the odyssey, unfortunately.

Q. When was the Grand Ole Opry founded?

A. The Grand Ole Opry was created in 1925 and began as a weekly radio program that featured traditional "country" music, including folk songs and classic mountain tunes. In 1939, the show moved to NBC radio, where it reached tens of thousands of listeners across the country. During the 1950s, the Opry was one of the nation's favorite radio programs. With every song played on the Opry stage broadcast across America, Nashville solidified its spot as the country music capital of the world.

Q. Who were some notable Grand Ole Opry performers?

A.

Hank Williams: By the mid-1930s, Hank Williams's legendary music career was well underway and would astonish everyone for years to come. Despite 12 number one songs, including "Hey Good Lookin'," Williams battled

alcoholism, which almost cost him a chance at the Opry. Producers couldn't bear not to feature Williams, however, and the country star joined the cast in 1949. He was called back for six encores the first time he performed. Williams died at age 29.

Patsy Cline: From humble beginnings came Patsy Cline, one of the most recognizable voices in country music. In 1957, Cline made her first national television appearance on *Arthur Godfrey's Talent Scouts*, singing what would become her first hit song, "Walkin' After Midnight." Three years later, Cline achieved a lifelong dream when she became a member of the Opry. Tragically, however, Cline died in a plane crash in 1963, just five years after her popularity snowballed.

Minnie Pearl: An upper-class girl from Tennessee, Sarah Colley decided to skip the debutante balls and formal education to pursue the vaudeville circuit. Colley created the character of Minnie Pearl after witnessing the brassy demeanor of a mountain lady during an amateur comedy show in 1936. When she joined the Opry in 1940, 28-year-old Colley had no idea she would spend the next 50 years in show business performing as Minnie Pearl and wearing her trademark straw hat with the $1.98 price tag still attached.

Dolly Parton: As a young girl growing up in the heart of Appalachia, Dolly Parton sang like a bird and even wrote her own songs modeled after the folksy tunes she learned from her parents. After appearing on a televised talent show, she was booked at the Opry in 1959 at the tender age of 13. Parton recorded steadily during the 1960s, but it wasn't until 1967 that her career skyrocketed when she was cast on the *Porter Wagoner Show*. Parton has recently returned to her roots, recording several critically acclaimed bluegrass albums.

Roy Acuff: In the 1930s and 1940s, no one sold more country music records than Roy Acuff. In 1938, this warbler became a regular performer and emcee on the Grand Ole Opry radio program. Known as the "King of Country Music," his performance of "The Great Speckled

Bird" changed the Opry forever—until then singers usually played second fiddle to the band.

Deford Bailey: When Deford Bailey was growing up in rural Tennessee, his parents gave him a harmonica, and history was made. Bailey's ability with the "harp" was unrivaled, and after he moved to Nashville, a few lucky breaks got him gigs playing on radio shows. In 1927, those breaks helped him land a spot on the Opry—without a formal audition. Bailey was the first African American included in the Opry cast and was one of the highest-paid stars of his day.

Loretta Lynn: Everyone's favorite "coal miner's daughter" joined the Opry after getting married, having four kids, and signing a recording contract—all before age 25. Lynn and her husband Mooney distributed (largely by hand) her first single, "I'm a Honky Tonk Girl," and through word of mouth and steady airplay, the single reached number 14 on the country charts in 1960. That impressive debut got Lynn her first appearance at the Opry that year, which boosted her career to the next level. She would go on to have dozens of megahits by blending her country girl image with some potent subject matter, such as birth control and deadbeat husbands. *Coal Miner's Daughter*, Lynn's autobiography, was made into an Academy Award-winning movie in 1980.

Johnny Cash: The people on this list are all titans of the country music world, but few are as well known as Johnny Cash, who has a place in both the Country Music Hall of Fame and the Rock and Roll Hall of Fame. The "Man in Black" joined the Opry in 1956 following the  success of his hit single "I Walk the Line." But he only stuck around for two years. Though Cash would battle addiction, a bitter divorce, and several career missteps, his popularity surged in the 1960s and again in the 1990s before his death in 2003.

Q. Who designed the Guggenheim Museum in New York City?

A. Architect Frank Lloyd Wright. Wright, who focused on designing buildings in harmony with nature and their environment, designed more than 1,000 structures and completed 500 works, including office buildings, churches, schools, skyscrapers, private residences, and museums. The American Institute of Architects called

Wright "the greatest American architect of all time." The renowned modern-art museum opened in 1959 and features many pieces from Solomon Guggenheim's personal collection.

Q. What is Marfa?

A. Perched in the high desert a ways north of the Mexican border and four hours from the nearest airport, at first glance Marfa looks like many small Texas towns—dusty, hot, and underpopulated. But Marfa is anything but ordinary. For starters, it's home to the mysterious Marfa Lights, which bring thousands of visitors to town annually to witness unexplained lights in the night sky. Then there's the iconic "Reata," the set for the movie

Giant, filmed there in the 1950s. Film buffs also know Marfa as the place where *No Country for Old Men* and *There Will Be Blood* were filmed.

But chief among its attractions is Marfa's thriving art scene, a cultural phenomenon that has put this sleepy town on the world map. With a year-round population of more than 2,000, it boasts more than 15 art galleries and artists' studios, several arts-oriented foundations, a growing community of working artists, and some of the most mind-boggling modern art pieces to be found anywhere.

Perhaps the town's literarily inspired name foreshadowed its future as an arts destination. Founded as a railroad watering stop in the mid-19th century and named for a character in a Dostoevsky novel, by the mid-1970s Marfa was down-at-the-heels and headed nowhere—and then artist Donald Judd arrived.

The Desert Blooms
Judd, a minimalist artist from New York, was in search of an expansive setting for the oversize art he and his colleagues were creating. He hit upon a former army post, Fort D.A. Russell, and over a few years bought up most of its 340 acres and, indeed, much of the town itself. Barracks, warehouses, gymnasiums, artillery sheds, hangars, and houses all were renovated and became home to dramatic art installations.

The Dia Foundation assisted Judd in his vision, and when it ran out of money, he formed his own Chinati Foundation. While Judd believed passionately that art needed to be displayed in suitable settings, he was not particularly concerned about whether the public actually came to see it. So, Marfa's growing importance to the art world was very hush-hush for years, until the Chinati Foundation started to promote Judd's legacy after his death in 1994.

Artists Begin to Colonize

By the early 1990s, as Judd's extraordinary complex became known to the rest of the world, more artists and art lovers flocked to Marfa. The extraordinary desert light, the quiet, the serene landscape, and Judd's inspiration drew people to Marfa. Soon, bookstores, coffee houses, and fine restaurants came, galleries opened, and artist studios bloomed. Newspapers, art magazines, and, of course, realtors took note.

Today, in addition to its full-time community of artists, more than 10,000 people visit Marfa annually to see Judd's work and other Chinati Foundation projects. Another organization, the Judd Foundation, manages still more facilities, including the house where Judd lived. The Lannan Foundation provides in-residence writers space and time to write. And at the Ballroom, an eclectic mix of art, performance art, and music is on the bill.

The work of artists such as Dan Flavin, John Chamberlain, John Wesley, Ilya Kabakov, Richard Long, Claes Oldenberg, and Coosje van Bruggen—huge works in aluminum, concrete, and neon—is seen to its most dramatic advantage set in repurposed buildings or outdoors in the wide-open spaces of the Big Bend. Judd's own installation of hundreds of large aluminum cubes set inside two enormous buildings is perhaps the most eye-catching. Also appealing is a Prada store, or what looks like one, anyway. Artists Michael Elmgreen and Ingar Dragset built a mock-up of the high-end chain store but sealed it tight, so it would always appear to be abandoned.

On a visit to Marfa in 2006, singer David Byrne found the town's vibe appealing. He blogged, "Marfa is in a dry flat area in between these outcroppings that you reach after winding through various hills and canyons. In some ways it is a typical small Texan town with a beautiful old central courthouse, a train track running through the middle, grain and cattle loading facilities . . . but that's where the ordinariness ends."

Q. ■ Which American writer spoke at Bill Clinton's first presidential inauguration?

A. ■ Maya Angelou. Best known for her prose, which includes the book *I Know Why the Caged Bird Sings*, Angelou is also a poet, playwright, editor, actress, director, and teacher. President Clinton commissioned her to write a poem for his 1993 inauguration. The poem, "On the Pulse of Morning," garnered as much attention for its content as for Angelou's reading at the inaugural ceremony.

Q. ■ How did the Smithsonian Institution come about?

A. ■ Perhaps no American museum is as well-known and beloved as the Smithsonian Institution's complex of art, science, history, and zoological museums in Washington, D.C.

In 1835, an unknown, illegitimate Englishman named James Smithson died, childless but not penniless. He had inherited a substantial estate from his parents—one of royal blood and the other a duke. In death he left the world a magnificent gift: an endowment for an American institution "for the increase and diffusion of knowledge among men"—the Smithsonian Institution.

Smithson's motives behind his unusual bequest remain a mystery. He never visited the United States, and there is little evidence that he ever even wrote to any American. Illegitimate son of the Duke of Northumberland, he may have felt slighted by a British society that deprived him of the privileges of a "legitimate" ducal heir. Or he may have taken a far-off interest in the bustling new democracy in which ideas and industry appeared to rule the day.

Whatever his motives, Smithson's offer of 100,000 gold sovereigns was too enticing for the young republic to refuse. U.S. President Andrew Jackson urged Congress to accept Smithson's gift, and upon congressional approval, the British gold was recast into 508,318 Yankee dollars.

Now What?

Having accepted the money, the nation faced an important question: "What do we do with it?"

Initially, Congress leaned toward using Smithson's gold to establish a national university. Plans for an institution specializing in the classics, science, or teaching skills were all proposed and rejected in turn. Other ideas— a national observatory, a laboratory, a museum, or a library—drew both support and opposition from the divided legislature. So the deadlocked Congress settled the matter by avoiding the issue entirely, leaving it to the Smithsonian's board of directors to determine the direction of the new institution.

America's Attic

The first proceeds were used for a building that would house the many tasks assigned to the new institution— teaching, experimenting, and exhibiting to the public. The building, located on the National Mall and now known as "the Castle," was designed in the medieval revival style, reminiscent of the ancient universities of James Smithson's homeland.

While the research and scientific functions of the Smithsonian grew steadily after the 1855 completion of the Castle, it was the national collection of odds and ends that  captured the public's mind and earned the Smithsonian its reputation as "America's attic." Fueled by the great American explorations of the Arctic, Antarctic, and interior regions of the United States, the Smithsonian's holdings grew from a small collection of pressed flora and preserved animal specimens to an assemblage that required the construction of a new building, the United States National Museum, in 1881.

Today, more than 170 years after Smithson died, the institute that bears his name comprises 19 museums, 4 research centers, a zoo, and a library research system. It is the largest single museum complex on the globe. From the fabled Hope Diamond to the historic Wright Flyer, from George Washington's dress sword to the original Kermit the Frog, the Smithsonian Institution pulls together the best of America's history and many relics of the world in which we live. Twenty-three million visitors per year grace its collection (an astounding 136.9 million objects) and its museums.

Q. **What 1960s song inspired a dance craze of the same name?**

A. Chubby Checker's number one song "The Twist" inspired the dance craze of the same name. The Twist was the first modern dance style that did not require a partner, and couples did not have to touch each other while dancing. Soon everyone was jumping on the bandwagon with a Twist record: Joey Dee and The Starliters reached number one with "The Peppermint Twist," while Sam Cooke was "Twistin' the Night Away."

Q. Where and what was Tin Pan Alley?

A. Tin Pan Alley is a block of row houses on West 28th Street in Manhattan. From the 1880s to the 1950s, this area produced the most famous songs in American pop music. During these years, passersby could hear music coming from these buildings. Newspaperman Monroe Rosenfeld coined the term Tin Pan Alley after hearing the dissonant sound of multiple composers simultaneously pounding on pianos in the area, or so the story goes. The area has been called Tin Pan Alley ever since.

Renowned lyricists from the era read like a veritable who's who of American music: Clarence Williams, Irving Berlin, Hoagy Carmichael, Cole Porter, and Irving Caesar merely scrape the surface of talent falling under the Tin Pan Alley banner. In the days when a song's popularity was determined by how many copies of sheet music it sold, immensely popular songs such as Al Jolson's "Swanee" and Shirley Temple's "Animal Crackers in My Soup" (lyrics for both were penned by Caesar) ensured that the new art form would not only survive, but thrive. When Caesar died in 1996 at the advanced age of 101, his passing marked the end of the original group of Tin Pan Alley lyricists. Nevertheless, the musical style lives on—a fact evidenced famously (if rather bizarrely) in 1985 with rocker David Lee Roth's cover of Caesar's "Just a Gigolo."

Q. Who wrote *Uncle Tom's Cabin*?

A. When Harriet Beecher Stowe was introduced to President Abraham Lincoln, as the story goes, he said, "So, you're the little woman who wrote the book that started this great war." There's no question that few elements fueled the flames of hate across the country as much as *Uncle Tom's Cabin* did. Stowe's story of Tom, a saintly black slave, and the difficult life he and his fellow slaves must endure, earned either praise or condemnation. Abolitionists across the North thought it was brilliant and oh, so true. Southern critics, however, complained that it was completely inaccurate in how it portrayed plantation life.

Borrowing from Real Life

Stowe was a dedicated abolitionist who was more concerned about illustrating the evils of slavery than creating an accurate view of life on the plantation. Although she lived in Cincinnati, Ohio, for 18 years, just across the river from the slave state of Kentucky, she had little actual experience with Southern plantations. The information in most of her book was taken either from abolitionist literature or her own imagination. Stowe was researching a series of articles she intended to write when she heard about a slave woman who escaped from her masters in Kentucky across a frozen Ohio River. She immediately realized that she could use such a scene in a book. One of the most exciting parts of *Uncle Tom's Cabin* features Eliza, the slave heroine, escaping across the ice.

A Publishing Sensation

Uncle Tom's Cabin first appeared in 1851, serialized in the abolitionist newspaper *National Era*. Its popularity there led to the book's publication as a complete work the next year. It was an instant success, selling ten thousand copies in the first week and more than three hundred thousand by the end of its first year. *Uncle Tom's Cabin* had even greater popularity in Britain, where more than one million copies sold within a year. Stowe exposed the general public to an issue that most knew very little about. But the book didn't simply educate its readers— it also provoked heated debates in state and federal legislatures.

Interestingly, given today's negative meaning of the term *Uncle Tom*, the character in Stowe's book demonstrated strength and traits that were quite heroic. In one instance, when ordered to whip a sickly female slave, Tom refuses and suffers the lash himself. His wicked master, Simon Legree, ultimately kills him because he will not betray two runaway slaves. When Legree tries to have the information beaten out of him, Tom goes to his death without revealing a thing.

Not Controversial Enough?
As shocking as a lot of people found *Uncle Tom's Cabin*, many—particularly radical abolitionists—didn't think the book went far enough in denouncing slavery. Others, usually those who lived in the South, condemned the book as grossly exaggerated. One of Stowe's admirers was William Lloyd Garrison, the editor of an abolitionist newspaper called *The Liberator*. "I estimate the value of antislavery writing by the abuse it brings," he wrote to tell her. "Now all the defenders of slavery have let me alone and are abusing you."

Q. What publication sent Henry Morton Stanley in search of Dr. David Livingstone in 1871?

A. The *New York Herald* sent Stanley on his quest to find Dr. Livingstone. When he came upon the missionary near Lake Tanganyika in south-central Africa in 1871, Stanley claimed to have greeted Livingstone with the words, "Dr. Livingstone, I presume?" The words have been ingrained in American culture ever since.

Q. Did American film pioneer Edwin S. Porter shoot his groundbreaking 1903 western, *The Great Train Robbery* in Hollywood, California?

A. No. Director Edwin S. Porter shot his masterpiece entirely in West Orange, New Jersey, at Thomas Edison's studio (called the "Black Maria") and on location. Most of the earliest American films were produced in studios in New Jersey, New York, or Chicago before the industry moved to the West Coast. In fact, Hollywood didn't see its first actual movie studio until 1911.

Thomas Edison called his studio the Black Maria (the slang term for a police wagon) because he thought it looked like a police wagon.

Q. Did Elvis really invent rock and roll?

A. We appreciate the skepticism implied by the "really" in this question. Can any single person have invented rock? And even if so, would Elvis Presley be that person? Gallons of intellectual blood have been spilled on this question, and we're going to spill a few more right here.

Elvis did invent rock and roll . . . sort of . . . maybe . . . in a way. If you define rock as a peculiarly American form of pop music that combines blues and country structures and riffs with aggressive—even distorted—guitars and edgy topics like love, lust, cars, and parties, then he definitely did not. Lots of folks were playing that tune several years before Elvis—a fact that Elvis himself happily acknowledged.

Queue up Jackie Brenston's "Rocket 88," and you'll see what we mean. Lots of folks consider that 1951 tune—written by Ike Turner—the birth of rock. Or you can go back to 1948 and Arthur Smith's "Guitar Boogie"—the first national hit to feature an electric guitar—as a watershed. Or it could have been Fats Domino's 1949 tune "The Fat Man," which historian Piero Scaruffi refers to as "certainly . . . a new kind of boogie." All of these songs have an indisputable rockin' quality that seems to differ from previous rhythm-and-blues or "race" music (so-called because of its black practitioners). They are fast, aggressive, rockin'—and Elvis was barely 13 when the first of them came out.

But if you do not define rock in purely musical terms—if you define it as a cultural phenomenon that was an amalgam of black and white influence and interest—then you can call Elvis the inventor. Better yet, let's call him "the right talent at the right time."

Certain critics excoriate Elvis and his handlers for this. Starting with his 1954 version of Arthur Crudup's "That's All Right Mama," historians have hammered Elvis for doing what popular musicians have done since the beginning of time: borrow from each other in an effort to be, well, popular. Scaruffi calls Elvis "the ultimate white robber of black hits," as if something as freewheeling as American roots music should respect vague, unwritten, idealistic, and narrow-minded notions of intellectual property.

Elvis himself never claimed to have invented rock, as historians have pointed out, and his cover of the Crudup tune was all in a day's work. In fact, Elvis was a devoted student of black gospel and R&B from childhood, and he combined his deep knowledge of those styles with his own spectacular (admit it!) talent to create a tune that's fantastic, no matter what your politics.

If you want to pinpoint when black and white first came together in a way that truly rocked—and defined the multicultural element of rock—then Elvis is your man, and "Mama" is your tune.

Q. How did National Geographic begin?

A. Little has changed at National Geographic since its inception, when a bunch of trailblazing academics, adventurers, and entrepreneurs united in the simple desire to spread their love of knowledge and discovery.

National Geographic is a challenge to classify: It walks like a duck, but it doesn't really quack like one. Most know National Geographic only through its monthly publication, *National Geographic* magazine. Yet the magazine is only the tip of a very large iceberg. National Geographic is actually a blanket term for the National Geographic Society, a nonprofit organization that funds scientific research and educational programs and is involved with projects that range from educating the public about global poverty to funding scientific research that seeks to end poverty.

National Geographic is scientific, yet its magazine targets everyday readers. The magazine's articles are based on scholarship, yet they read like creative journalism. National Geographic funds research,  yet it is not an academic institution. National Geographic's hodgepodge of media subdivisions, from television channels to documentaries to radio shows, has the flavor of a pop culture empire—but with philanthropic goals. In short, National Geographic is one of those rare organizations that, through its ability to resist society's typically rigid divisions, is also able to transcend them.

This combination of lowbrow and highbrow was built into National Geographic from the beginning. The Society was founded mostly by academics, yet their goal was to include everybody, no matter their education level, in the pursuit of knowledge. In 1888, scientists and adventurers from all over the United States met at the Cosmos Club in Washington, D.C., right across from the White House. Included in this group were teachers, lawyers, geographers explorers of various stripes, and even military officers. All of these individuals were united by their passion to discover truths about the world, whether they be the location of the world's highest mountain peak or the customs of a different culture.

In those days, much of the earth was uncharted territory. Colonialism had only recently introduced the world to the vast multiplicity of human culture. The founders of the National Geographic Society wanted people to be informed of the exciting new discoveries that were taking place. The founders resolved that inclusion in the society should be "on as broad and liberal a basis in regard to qualifications for membership as is consistent with its own well-being and the dignity of the science it represents." The National Geographic Society was officially incorporated on January 27, 1888.

The first issue of *National Geographic Magazine* (later shortened to just *National Geographic*) was published nine months after the Society was founded. The founders decided that a magazine would be the best way to educate the public about scientific findings. Unlike academic journals with their obscure language and esoteric references, *National Geographic Magazine* was intended to unite people in a curiosity for the world. Gilbert Hovey Grosvenor, Alexander Graham Bell's son-in-law, was the magazine's first editor, and from the outset, he established an all-encompassing criteria for geographic knowledge as "embracing nations, people, plants, animals, birds, fish. It enters into history, science, literature, and even the languages."

National Geographic's renown for publishing startlingly beautiful photographs commenced in 1905, when Grosvenor had a deadline and 11 blank pages to fill. On a whim, he published 11 pages' worth of photographs of Tibet, and from there on out made photographic journalism a focus of the publication. The first issue of *National Geographic* was sent to 165 people; today, *National Geographic* is published in more than 30 languages, with a circulation of more than 8 million. The National Geographic Channel has more than 65 million viewers, and the National Geographic Society is one of

the world's largest and most influential nonprofit
organizations.

Q. What legendary playwright choked to death on a bottle cap?

A. Legendary playwright Tennessee Williams died in
1983 as a result of choking on the cap of an eye-
drop bottle, though drugs and alcohol may have been
involved as well. Williams was a serious hypochondriac
obsessed with his own sickness and death. He was shy
and equally afraid of both failure and success.

Q. Whose 1953 novel about censorship was censored itself?

A. Ray Bradbury. Reportedly, Bradbury wrote
Fahrenheit 451 in the basement of the UCLA
library on a pay-by-the-hour typewriter. Ironically, the
story examines censorship, but unbeknownst to
Bradbury, his publisher released a censored edition in
1967, nixing all profanity so the book would be safe for
distribution in schools. A school in Mississippi banned
the book in 1999 for the use of the very words Bradbury
insisted be put back into the book when it was reprinted.

Q. Is a soft drink a soda or a pop?

A. This is the kind of question that could incite an
all-out riot, depending on where you live. Say

"soda" in Nebraska and you're sure to get some crooked stares. Ask for a "pop" in New Jersey, and you just might get a pop in the nose. But just where are the lines drawn in this super silly, super carbonated war of words?

That's just what California Institute of Technology student Alan McConchie intended to find out. For a 1993 college project, the future computer programmer and part-time linguist created a "Pop vs. Soda" Web site, asking visitors to enter their hometown zip code and soft drink descriptor of choice. The votes were then tabulated and plotted on a North America map with color-coded dots— green dots for pop and blue dots for soda.

The results? The Midwest turned out to be pop central; green dots swarmed the map from Wyoming to West Virginia. Oddly though, areas around St. Louis and Milwaukee went blue, pulling for soda, along with a mass of voters concentrated in the Northeast and California.

If you thought a national Internet election could settle this fizzy fistfight once and for all, your Fanta's gone flat. The votes continue to be tabulated on McConchie's site, and they have been fairly evenly split between pop and soda. (You can see the data for yourself at popvssoda.com.)

If you look at the Web site, you'll note that not everyone voted for pop or soda. Where are these rogue votes coming from? Down South. (Aren't those Southerners always the ones messing up elections?) In places like Alabama, Arkansas, Louisiana, Georgia, Mississippi, Texas, and parts of Florida, among others, a soft drink is neither a pop nor a soda—it's a coke. A Coca-Cola's a coke. A Pepsi's a coke. A Mountain Dew's a coke. A Sunkist Orange is a coke. It's important to note that some people in this part of the country are also known to refer to their carbonated beverages as sody pop.

But hey, whatever floats your sarsaparilla, right? We all have our local liquid refreshment lingo, and it's clear we're pretty passionate about it. Now would someone please tell those backward Bostonians that a soft drink is not called a tonic?

Q. Where did corn flakes come from?

A. Battle Creek, Michigan. That's where Dr. J. H. Kellogg ran what he called a *sanitarium*, dedicated to healthy living. He and his brother, W. K. Kellogg, were interested in finding new foods to support that goal. Completely by accident in 1894, the brothers discovered a way to create toasted wheat flakes, and they started experimenting with other grains. The corn variety became quite popular, and the brothers started to sell it commercially. They fought over the recipe— W. K. wanted to add sugar, while J. H. wanted the cereal to remain pure and be sold as a health food. Ultimately W. K. started his own company, Kellogg's, which today is known to breakfast lovers nationwide.

Q. What city inspired the names of the properties in the Monopoly board game?

A. Atlantic City, New Jersey. Although the origins of the game have been disputed in court, in 1934, Charles Darrow, an out-of-work salesman, sold the game featuring Atlantic City street names to Parker Brothers. One error was never corrected, however. Marven Gardens, an area just south of Atlantic City, was misspelled *Marvin Gardens* and remains in the game to this day.

Q. Who is known as the "father of the modern detective story"?

A. Edgar Allan Poe, one of the most influential American writers of the 19th century. Among his most famous works are "The Raven" (a poem published 1845) and "The Tell-Tale Heart" (a short story, 1843). Poe has also been called the "Master of the Macabre."

Q. Who are considered the leaders of the Beat Generation?

A. Jack Kerouac, Allen Ginsberg, and William S. Burroughs. The "Beat Generation" is the name given to a generation of poets, writers, artists, and activists during the 1940s and '50s. The name originated in 1948 when Jack Kerouac told a magazine interviewer that his generation was "beat, man." Kerouac later said beat was short for "beatific." Kerouac suffered through six years of rejections before his most famous novel, *On the Road*, was finally published in 1957. The thinly veiled autobiography recounts Kerouac's travels across the United States and Mexico in the late 1940s.

Q. Who created Superman?

A. In the 1930s, Ohio high school student Jerry Siegel wrote a story about a man from another planet who was unassuming by day but secretly had amazing powers. His friend Joe Shuster illustrated it. The pair had no luck selling the idea for several years.

Q. Which silent-film star was at the center of one of Hollywood's first scandals in 1921?

A. Roscoe "Fatty" Arbuckle. Arbuckle was a greatly successful on-screen comedian and even mentored the likes of Charlie Chaplin, but after a woman claimed that Arbuckle had raped her and died shortly thereafter of injuries believed to have been caused by Arbuckle, the funny-man's days were done. He was eventually cleared of all charges, but it was too late; the damage had been done, and Arbuckle didn't set foot on the silver screen for ten years.